T0063080

NO NAME WILL DO

Yellow Mouse

Order this book online at www.trafford.com
or email orders@trafford.com

Most Trafford titles are also available at major online book retailers.

© Copyright 2014 Yellow Mouse.
All rights reserved. No part of this publication may be reproduced, stored in a retrieval
system, or transmitted, in any form or by any means, electronic, mechanical, photocopying,
recording, or otherwise, without the written prior permission of the author.

No Name Will Do was written 1980 and 1984 and edited in1986 and 1988 by Yellow Mouse
(PIE: GHEL-MUS), a.k.a. Michael Hillegass (registered name), a.k.a. Yam Hailagaz.

Scripture quotations marked KJV are from the Holy Bible, King James Version
(Authorized Version). First published in 1611. Quoted from the KJV Classic
Reference Bible, Copyright © 1983 by The Zondervan Corporation.

Printed in the United States of America.

ISBN: 978-1-4907-4115-4 (sc)
ISBN: 978-1-4907-4117-8 (hc)
ISBN: 978-1-4907-4116-1 (e)

Library of Congress Control Number: 2014912113

Because of the dynamic nature of the Internet, any web addresses or links contained in
this book may have changed since publication and may no longer be valid. The views
expressed in this work are solely those of the author and do not necessarily reflect the
views of the publisher, and the publisher hereby disclaims any responsibility for them.

Any people depicted in stock imagery provided by Thinkstock are models,
and such images are being used for illustrative purposes only.
Certain stock imagery © Thinkstock.

Trafford rev. 10/28/2014

 www.trafford.com

North America & international
toll-free: 1 888 232 4444 (USA & Canada)
fax: 812 355 4082

Dedicated to June Street

PREFACE

What am I trying to do herein? It is my purpose to communicate the existence of a (singular) truth: one concept that I believe has been forgotten— lost—by the people of the modern world. There are many statements and products of my life herein, but they are all merely tools to this one end. It cannot be named for the reader; this truth can only be experienced. But awareness of a concept is a necessary ingredient before experience of it can occur. All words are merely metaphors—none are sacred—it is the concepts that MAY be sacred. Thus these words or ideas that I have used are not sacred; any and all of them may be discounted or discarded. If you would claim that one of my ideas is wrong, I would agree so that no diversion or distraction from my central and sole purpose may occur. I have studiously refrained from focusing on religion, psychology, science, comparative cultures, etc., as being such distractions. Likewise, I have refused to follow the many side trails left dangling herein. There are too many good books on mysticism for me to repeat all those messages or even to try to build a bibliography. I refer the reader to the entire world of the written word.

For those who hate puns, I apologize for the title's terrible triple, but it says such a bookful. I encourage the reader to participate during reading by taking notes, disagreeing, arguing, and getting mad at me. I have capitalized several words here and there, intending to tweak the thinking process. All word definitions come from the Proto-Indo-European (PIE) at some time between 3000 and 8000 BC (*American Heritage Dictionary of the English Language*).

Thanks to the thousands of so-called workers, criminals, delinquents, bums, cowboys, thinkers, writers, and ordinary people who have lived this life and been willing to share it with me.

CHAPTER I

People have been reading and studying the scriptures for centuries, always in search of something—something ineffable, indefinable, apparently unreachable. They call it TRUTH. And every man seems to have a separate and distinct truth. If the student were not so terribly centered around her own needs, problems, and search, s/he might discover the TRUTH: that words are the problem. We are forever trying to communicate by the use of weak ambiguous terms, like "truth." Truth has been seen by many people over the centuries, and they have handed on what they have seen (at least what they said they have seen). People have spent their energies (and their lives) attacking or defending these views. But only a few have been able to look at the evidence calmly without a set—a goal—already in mind.

Great students, leaders, saints, gurus, etc., have passed on to us their views. Naturally, each was and is culturally conditioned. Metaphors used in one culture and time are not understood fully by other cultures and other times. Instead of being bound to the word usage of an ancient time and place, we must realize that the words were only metaphors, yet that every metaphor may be of use to us since it was once of use to those of another time and place. Theologians should be our greatest of resources, but all have proved to be biased to their own specific view.

If we take ourselves out of all this—our own cultural conditioning—and, with an unbiased mind, study these metaphysics, religions, mysticisms, spiritualisms, etc., we will find a common core of belief. There is more than one concept to this core, so let us start with the concept that each and every one of the great religions agree on one truth: that THERE IS ONLY ONE WAY, *THE* WAY—ONLY THIS WAY—THE WAY. Although they all seem to be talking about different ways, that distracts us from the central truth: THERE IS TRULY ONLY ONE WAY. And each of these systems is trying to tell us that.

With that as a starting point, let us note that most religions take words to be sacred. WRONG! The written word is merely a symbol. But it is not a symbol for an idea; it is a symbol for a sound. The spoken word came first—before the written word or hieroglyphics. Words are sounds, and they are used as pointers, labels, and symbols to indicate ideas. Thus, at the root, sign language, signs, and spoken words (and ultimately the written word) are all symbols for meanings, ideas, and concepts. Words have no meaning in and of themselves other than what is assigned (consciously or unconsciously) to them by people. Not only is a word meaningless by itself, but there can be no spoken sound unless a human speaks it and thereby places MEANING thereon (and s/he who listens places HIS own meaning thereon). The subject is not, "What does a word mean?" but rather, "What word will AGREEABLY symbolize MY concept? " What are truly sacred are the concepts themselves.

Which brings us to esotericism. "Exo-" is a prefix for "outer" used to indicate patent, apparent, surficial; whereas "eso-" indicates "inner," hidden, latent, beneath, not clear, unobvious. Most religions depend (yes, "depend") on exotericism in order to propagate their dogmas and doctrines (their truths) so that all is clear, patent, exoteric. Thus individuality automatically becomes suppressed for the troops must be able to know and believe in something common for the group. Thus truth becomes secondary to ideology. The worst offense is the shift from the true truth to that now defined by the ideology—which is, by definition, ALWAYS CLEARLY FALSE, no matter what or whose doctrine, dogma, or ideology. The subject herein is not "truth" but esotericism, which is the study of the hidden meanings behind the symbols: the concepts of truth that exist IN this world, IN all ideologies, but not OF them.

Esotericism lives primarily because of the "aHA!" phenomena: the rush of bliss and joy in the individual known as enlightenment. When multiple meanings are conjoined and make a new, the student is overcome with the obviousness of what could not be seen at all previously. Hebrew, Arabic, and Aramaic alphabets (the absence of vowels) have brought people direct experience of esotericisms. But such mystical non-absolute knowledge is frightening to adolescents:

children requiring certainty (absolutes) to cover their fears. Since man is not a clearly apprehended subject (s/he is full of ambiguities and ambivalences), esotericism is THE ONLY WAY (the ONEWAY) to understand mankind and hir world. So let us join in a search for the real truth in the mysteries and vast labyrinths of mankind.

Psychology uses the technique of peeling the onion to discover what is hidden beneath the surface of a person. This is a method common to all religions, metaphysics, and psychologies. This exposes another truth: we have in ourselves the power to discover what we ourselves are all about. We have remarkable tools and techniques for studying the layers of the onion. But when we pull our heads out of the set of layer-studying, we will be forced to ask, when we have peeled off the last of the layers, WHAT WILL WE FIND? The existential terror is that NOTHING is at the center of the onion. Psychology and the study of oneself using psychological technique are all about the intricacies of the various layers. But it has failed to deal with the problem: WHAT IS AT THE CENTER of a human being?

EXISTENCE is there.

EXIST = EXISTERE (Lat.): to exist, emerge, come forth
      = EX: out of + SISTERE = to take a position or stand firm
      = STA (PIE): to stand (> = which goes or evolves to)
      > that which stands, a place (where IT stands);
      > set up or erected (that which was caused to stand);
      > the state or status (the condition in which it stands)

THUS, EXISTENCE = (a) something stands out from the mists of CHAOS and takes a firm unyielding reality, OR (b) I project a firm and unchanging ORDER on that CHAOS and thus attain some known, certainty.

The existential problem lies at the core of being and not in the layers of the onion. The existentialists feel that it is the human fate to live a meaningless life because they have found NOTHING at the center. The psychologists and the existentialists are in agreement about one TRUTH: there is a center. For the one, it is irrelevant, and for the other, it is meaningless. Neither is correct, but they do point us to the truth that a center exists.

3

Let us define two concepts and use two words as symbols or labels to tag these concepts. One is the word "homo," the Latin word used by scientists to designate human kind, as in "homo sapiens": discerning man. Let's accept that our culture is dominated by scientists and scientistic thinking. Paleontology, anthropology, and archeology are the sciences that have dug (literally) into the records of mankind and have defined, refined, described, and pulled apart man's history, genesis, derivation, conditioning, etc. In all their studies, they refer to that specific genus of life by their name: homo. I suggest that we accept that as THE CORRECT label, for they are the experts.

There has been a conflict in science between two ideas: free will and determinism. Scientists tell us that humanity is determined. But that thinking is fuzzy because of the use of the wrong label. What they mean is "homo," in which case they are correct since what they study IS "homo." "Homo" IS conditioned and IS determined in his responses to the environment. The purpose here is not to dig into this morass but to clarify in order to find truth. We must accept the evidence that homo is a determined animal. Look closely at that: IS MAN AN ANIMAL? The true answer can be found, but NOT IN THAT FORM of question. The problem is that the word "man" is ambivalent. "Homo" has a specific definition—and we have accepted it. We have already set "homo" to indicate exactly this concept. Is homo an animal? Obviously, YES, because we set up our definition that way. Thus it is absolute TRUTH that homo is a determined animal. A study of the applicable sciences will allow a student no other conclusion.

Now back to our train of thought. There is a center, and it is distinguishable from the layers of the onion. At the core, there is SOMETHING. At this point in our logic, we do not know WHAT it is, but we know that IT exists. We are not believing any of this; we know it. Now we see that "homo" and "man" are NOT synonymous. Great thinkers have told us for millennia that man has a free will and is NOT determined. And this has felt right to each one of us. Out of all this conflict, there comes a : "MAN" is something OTHER than homo; "homo + " perhaps. These words, merely symbols, symbolize different concepts. When we talk about "man," we are, by definition, NOT talking about "homo." We have not yet a full definition for "man," but we do know that in addition to "homo," there is a moreness that has to do with whatever "man" is.

Let us coin another word here. First, because it has already been used; secondly, because it makes so much sense here. "Center" has been used for centuries in the mystical trade because it symbolizes so precisely what is desired. The center of a circle is the point from which the circle is described by its radius. The circle and all the space therein depends on the center for its existence and location. A point has no dimension other than location. A point is an abstract concept. It is left when all the visible portion of a circle is stripped away—and it is featureless, dimensionless, and even appears nonexistent. BUT IT IS THERE (location). WHAT it is is unknown—BUT IT IS. So let us use this label "center" to indicate the core of being at the center of homo's existence. That core is also something more, and like a center, it too is dimensionless: WITHOUT DEFINITION.

"KNOW THYSELF" is the admonition of old; when you discover who you are, you will have discovered God. But that is mere dogma. Analyzing the words, however, it becomes clear that there *must* be a subject who does the knowing (i.e., the KNOWER), and there must be an object that is KNOWN. This points out clearly that there is a duality inherent in the language.

So where are we then? All religions insist that there is but ONEWAY to truth. Words are only symbols, and we manipulate them. We must look under the dogmatic surface for the hidden meanings in order to obtain enlightenment. Although psychology deals with the onion (a necessary work), yet what is at the center has to do with the core of being, about which we are all involved (revolved). Otherwise, we have to deal with nothingness and meaninglessness. Although "homo" is a determined animal, yet there is something more referred to as "man." And the differences are to be found at that centerpoint of existence.

CHAPTER II

We must distinguish between semantics and linguistics. I do not wish to dig too deeply into this, but thinkers have been attacked many times as being semanticists—meaning that they are playing word games. Where semantics talks about word meaning, linguistics talks about why and how our language conditions our ways of thinking (and vice versa). If we are going to try to discover something about this ONEWAY, then we must know how our minds work. A tool, taken from Zen, is suggested: the aggressive *four*-letter word "WHO?"

In all these studies, we are forced to use certain pronouns. I say "I see." But WHO? sees? The see-er (seer) sees. WHO? is the seer? Do you see? WHO? is "you"?—or WHO? is "you"! This is ridiculously simple, but absolutely confusing to those who do not see. If there is "man" (homo) *and* "man" (homo + center), then we will always have a problem as to which one is being referred to when we say "I." "you," "we," etc. So whenever you say "I believe," you (WHO?) must accept this attack on your statement: WHO? is doing the action called believing? Is it the conditioned, dependent, determined animal called homo? Or is it something else? This word "WHO?" is a very important tool to be used carefully and correctly to remind self (WHO?) and others that they may not be in touch with what is actually happening. Linguistically, it is impossible to say "I" and indicate which concept is speaking (or being referred to). Thus the necessity of a continual awareness signal cued by the "WHO?" question, for the speaker may be confused or confusing who he means by "I."

And there is a second linguistic problem: materialism. When we refer to God, one is forced into confusion by the very fact that the word "God" is a NOUN. A noun is a thing. I am not referring to ANY belief system; I am referring to a linguistic truth: NOUNS REFER TO THINGS and are the subjects or objects of an action or verb. Thus, WE PERMIT "God" to be an actor or to be acted upon. Thus "God" is limited and cannot BE a power for "he" is NOT A VERB: "IT" is a noun. Unfortunate—for when we say "God is love,", we are pointing to two nouns across an equivalency: noun G equals noun L. So LOVE MUST BE A THING, also. We are trapped in our language with no way out. If you wish to find out about God, you ask "WHAT is IT?" "What" and "it" can ONLY refer to things (i.e., materialism). If we suppose God to be an energy flow, "it" is therefore NOT a thing, and a noun cannot be used to symbolize this concept. And then the question becomes unanswerable. Love is not a noun; "it" is a verb. We may say properly: God loves. But then love is separated from God. God DOES it (love), but love cannot be God. In this realm, we may end up with no nouns to make sentences out of. Homo may do an action called love, which makes sense since homo is a thing, an animal. What then is "man"? "It" too is a noun. But is the center of our being a THING? NO! For when we arrive at the center, by definition, we have left all the peels (things) behind. We have NO THING left to the circle other than the abstraction: location—and that only for where the circle (peels, things) once was.

Basically, at this point, we want to pause to understand clearly that our thinking is muddied by the presence of these linguistic problems inherent in our language. In order to find truth, we must be in control of our linguistic tools. It is the TRUTH: our Western languages have a materialistic set that forces on all of us that materialistic WAY of thinking and seeing. We won't get out of that set by wishing for it or in any other way. We must meet it head-on and expose it and deal, cope, with it—not complain about it.

*

IMAGINE = IMAGE = IMAGO: to picture to oneself
= IN + MAG (PIE): to make, knead
= MANGJAN: to knead together = MENGAN = MINGLE: MIX
THUS, INMAG = to make within: to fashion, knead or fit into an inner pattern.

7

THUS, IMAGE = inside the mind, to mix, knead, and make sensory inputs received, into a finished product.

"Imagination" is a label for some "thing." What concept does that label represent? Is "imagination" power, or is it hallucination? If one hallucinates that another wants to kill hir and therefore strikes first, then that hallucination has had a great deal of power. However, we object to the day-dreaming child in a classroom. Both examples point out that we all have ideological interests in this subject. So let's be careful and stick to an unbiased place. Thus we may ask whether the center, shushumna, chakras, nagual, tonal, sephirah, spirit, soul, or other ideational terms used in various esoteric metaphysics and religions are real, fictional, imaginary, hallucinatory, or MADE REAL by some process. If we care, we will attempt to determine whether they are real or not. A noun is a word symbolizing a thing, which, by definition (materialistically), is real. Is, therefore, hallucination real? If one believes strongly enough, does it become real? Here is not to answer these questions but to pose the problem of how the mind works and the existence of these linguistic traps. What if the list of items above were TRULY NOT NOUNS?
Roberto Assagioli's book *Psychosynthesis* indicated that the SELF can be experienced only when it makes itsSELF felt. He indicated that the center may not in fact exist, for we can know *it* only when it makes itself apparent by acting in, through, or on us. That makes it not a thing but a point of energy flow. When energy is turned off, it is nonexistent; "IT" IS NOT, for "IT" is NOT a THING. When turned on and flowing, it HAPPENS: it is an event, a phenomenon. Assagioli called this happening, the ACT of will—an action and not a thing. Our language does not allow us easily to discuss or even use these ideas about energy flows. We know everything about how to use electricity, but we don't know yet WHAT IT is. There you are again: "what" "it" is. And if "it" isn't a thing, we are in trouble. It is no wonder that we don't know WHAT electricity is, since it isn't a WHAT. It is an energy flow—TRUTH!

BELIEVE = BELEVEN (Mid. Eng.) = BELEFAN, GELEFAN (Old Eng.)
      from LEUBH (PIE): to care, desire, love
      = LEUBHO = LIUBAZ (Teut.):

(-AZ: s/he who or that which) is desired
= LEOF (Old Eng.): What I desire is dear, beloved to me
= LOVE (noun)
= LOUBH = LAUBO (Teut.) = LEAF (Old Eng.)
= LEAVE: approval given with pleasure for what
    is desired = permission
= GA-LAUBO (Teut.) = GELEAFA, BILEAFE (Old Eng.)
= GELAFEN, BELEFAN
= BELIEF (noun): approval in what pleases
    the mental act, condition, or habit (set?) of placing trust
    or confidence in something accepted as true
= GALAUBJAN (Teut.): to hold dear, esteem, trust
= GELEFEN, BILEFEN (Old Eng.) = BILEVEN = BELEVE
= BELIEVE: to accept, to credit as true,
    have confidence in, trust, to expect, or suppose trust
= LUBH = LUBHA = LUBO (Teut.) = LUFU (Old Eng.)
= LOVE (verb): an intense affectionate concern for,
    a strong fondness or enthusiasm for
= LUBHE = LIBERE (Lat.): to be dear or pleasing
= LIBIDO (Lat.): pleasure, desire, LIBIDO

THUS, BELIEVE = the mental act of placing confidence in, accepting or crediting something one holds dear, esteems, trusts, is pleasured by. The choice is by one's own authority and has nothing at all to do with whether that something is objectively true. Such arguments are merely rationalizations and projections for one's own pleasures.

When we deal internally with the human mind and ask the esoteric question about what people REALLY intend from the depths of their psyche when they believe—the answer we receive is much like to BELIEVE is to accept the truth that we very much desire to be true: a choice of commitment to that which we, BY DEFINITION, do NOT KNOW, objectively, as truth. If it were TRUTH, we could and would KNOW it and have no need for the operation called belief. Belief has to do with authority and ideology. Our dogma may be infant baptism, but our problem here is understanding the process of "how one believes," NOT "what is the truth." Herein, we are not interested in

ANYONE'S "beliefs, including our own. We are interested in what is known and carefully distinguishing that from all else.

For millennia, people have been raising their eyes to the heavens, pointing out there to "God." But that idea is conditioned on the understanding that the earth is flat. Each one looks up (to the sun?) and prays to the god(s) for help. Ever since Copernicus and Kepler, we have known a truth: the earth is a sphere; it is NOT flat. But have we yet accepted the consequences of that truth? If those who pray to God are standing on a spherical earth, then they are all pointing outward in differing directions. In the first instance of the flat earth, people point up toward a thing, but in the second, when they point everywhere, the concept of "God" changes from a thing (heaven was a place—a destination) to a cloud, an atmosphere, a milieu in which we "live, move, and have our being." It is no longer the God "out there," but becomes the God "right here": God with us.

And if we use another scientific truth: that we are made of cells, which are made of molecules arranged in lattices of various types and shapes, which are made of atoms, protons, electrons, etc., swimming in a vast space, then that "God" atmosphere, cloud, milieu is also WITHIN the atomic lattice of our existence. It has now become the GOD "WITHIN"—not the God "out there," but the God "in here." So I MUST conclude that God IS WITHIN ME and all others.

There is a second part to this "out there" thinking. In order for God to be "out there," there must be an observer here. Why? In order to observe something "out there," there must be someone "here" to do the pointing. In that scene, God and the observer are separated, alienated one from another. Thus the concept of God "out there" demands an authority here who tells us about what he sees "out there." That is a THING "out there": a material object: God in a place: heaven. This isn't belief, questionable suppositions; this is truth.

So now we have a God "in here." Can I be the observer (the authority) to do THIS POINTING for another? NO! This is not possible even if I wanted it that way very much. This "God" is a misty cloud that is OMNIPRESENT. I can peer into myself, but I cannot peer into you (even though I can peek beneath your surface). YOU must, of necessity, do your own peering and pointing for yourself. Remember, here we are pointing, not to a thing, a noun, but to an energy flow, a verb.

We have already seen one modern English linguistic problem: materialism. The reverse is best illustrated in the linguistic shift that occurred with the advent of science (circa 1800): gerunds. Western languages have used gerunds so long as to have forgotten that they are verbs and not nouns in certain vital usages. The word "being" is one of these. We use "being," as in "human being," in such a way that the "be-" and the "-ing" (see KING, page xxx) are made one. But a "Being" is NOT a THING. It is a happening, an event, something changing.

"Happening," "changing," "moving," "being," "shouting," "running," "hitting" are NOT nouns; they are action words: VERBS. They do NOT refer to THINGS; they refer to something that happens, changes, moves, shouts, runs, hits. Thus "snow happens," "life changes," "families move," "Harry shouts," "scatbacks run," and "batters hit." All these are actions, happenings, events.

A being thus is something that "bes," or "is." But "bes" implies "continue to be." When we look at a person standing still, we make the mistake of thinking that nothing is happening. But there is something very vital happening: s/he is *not* a thing, an inanimate object: S/HE IS ALIVE, LIVING, BE-ING. S/he is continuing to BE, to exist as a LIFE here and now. The necessary flow of energy that distinguishes hir from a dead body is flowing through hir and making hir what s/he is. Without that spark of energy, s/he would NOT BE— truly, nothing happening anymore. But so long as s/he BES, there is an event happening. An event so remarkable, so singular, so fantastic, that we MUST bow down and worship it. The spark of life, cosmic energy, God's power, the eternal force of the universe is entering hir somehow and keeping hir in BEING. That energy flowing through hir center IS GOD (verb). That human is not a being (a thing); S/HE IS *BEING*: an event in process.

What makes a human alive? What gives homo life? There is a spark of life within, which all men have pointed to as the center of their being. All peoples think about a creator and pray that life be theirs a little while longer. And if that spark is withdrawn, what will keep a person alive one moment longer? What is the difference between a body asleep and another freshly deceased? Nothing but the presence or absence of that spark of life. We cannot apprehend it or hold it in our hot little hands, but it makes ALL the DIFFERENCE.

*

AND just what is God? GOD = GOD (Old Eng.) = GUDAM (Teut.)
    = GHUTAZ (IE) = GHUT: call
      + AZ: (s/he who or that which) is called or invoked.
      from GHEUE (PIE): to call, invoke = GHUTAZ (Teut.)
    = GOT (Old Ger.) = GOTT (Ger.): god.
THUS, GOD is that which (S/HE, whoever) I, we, invoke, call to.
Incidentally, GOOD = GOD (Old Eng.)
    = GODAZ (Teut.): fitting, suitable = GHODH
    = GHEDH (PIE): to unite, join, fit.
THUS, "God" is not "good,"
nor is "good" good, but merely fitting, suitable.
(But to join, unite with God is good.)

So "God" is that which is called upon—in times of stress, no doubt. But the word does not tell us WHAT is called upon or WHO is invoked, merely that something IS invoked. Thus, to say "I call upon God" is to say "I call upon whatever I called upon," which says nothing, for it is cyclical and redundant. To say "'God is X" is false, for what we mean is that it is X that we invoke, call upon—X that is the target of our calling, invocation.

"ARE YOU GOD?" is an accusation.
"God" = (*a*) good and/or (*b*) the invoked.
(*a*) GOOD: If I am God and "God" IS "good,"
    and "God looked on hir creation and found it good."
    translates as "that which is good looked on what s/he created
    and discovered that it was good."
    which means: the good created good
    (and, by definition, there was no other choice)
    THUS, (*a*) I was created by God, and (*b*) I am good.
    Yes, it follows, God also being good: I am God.
(*b*) The INVOKED: If I am God, then I must invoke myself.
    Do I INVOKE ME?
    No, of course not. I invoke something outside myself.
    But externalizing an "out there" God is only
    a rationalization, a projection that is incorrect.

12

For what I value, believe is truth
(according to my own authority).
Thus, I do, naturally, invoke
my own values, beliefs, ego, being
—but that, by definition, is NOT God.
Then "I AM GOD" is redundant and cyclical for—
    "I, the invoked God, am [is] the invoked God"
says nothing at all.

God gave us the answer—s/he said merely "I AM—YAM!"
Then what do I, homo, invoke?   Homo, of course.
    And what (WHO?) does that "OTHER," YAM, MAN, invoke?
NO-THING, for s/he IS BEING.

"I," homo, am a shield covering YAM.
This whole organism is a shield that YAM, MAN thinks
s/he needs to protect hirself.
But WHAT S/HE IS is an illusion:
Homo is only what YAM dreams s/he is: projects.
And when YAM wakens, s/he KNOWS hirSelf to BE—BEING!

"God" is not a being (a thing), but a concept for which "God" is merely the label. We refer to "God" in many ways: fate, destiny, chance, nature, cosmic energy, love, truth, etc. These are all just words. But they are synonymous on two levels: they are all nouns, and they are all meaningless, even though we may have psychologically loaded all kinds of meanings onto them. These words all say: NO THING.

*

Do we really believe in ONEGOD ? We know that we invoke our own egos since they are our most important asset. But that way, there are millions of gods, just as there was once family gods for each and every family. If we truly are monotheists, then we are forced to ONEGOD and cannot deviate. This is not the problem that ONEGOD may have many names or distinguishing the many facets of ONEGOD. The monotheist may invoke only one "s/he

13

who is invoked," but it may not be the same "s/he who is invoked" someone else invokes. That conflict makes us aware that we are not monthesists. It is our unconscious loading of these words that subverts our conscious intention to be monotheistic.

There are many concepts for "God," but here is another truth about God: GOD *MUST* BE UNKNOWN. Mankind becomes more powerful than "God" and conquers "HIR" when s/he is able to define "HIR." When one KNOWS, it is the KNOWER who has the power and thus becomes God. Thus the authoritarian makes hirself into God: s/he invokes hirself. This is a basic problem for our life today: not only are we dominated by scientists (knowers) and conditioned into a materialistic world, but we are also all arrogant authoritarians. WE KNOW THE ANSWERS. "Science will solve all the problems of the world." THAT is arrogance, when you consider just how little we really do know. We construct a god and a religion, which reflects the world in which we live. So our God is a thing "out there" somewhere, estranged from us (and we alienated from hir) where we can deal with hir as an object and where s/he can't deal with us. That puts US (WHO?) in command.

Here we are using the word "center" to indicate that spark of life, the God within, the Buddha, the Christ (as distinguished from Jesus), the Christ-point, the point of contact between homo and the divinity: that something more that is "man." But we, homo, have no command, no control over that center. We can hardly grasp its existence since it is not a thing, and our language gives us no tools. What say we (WHO?) then? WHO? sees this center? The scientist cannot see a center or a Christ-point, thus s/he is correct to deny it, its existence, for it is NOT a thing, since scientists only study things. The center is only a location (point) where energy flows into our being and gives us life, mobility, energy—"in which we live, move, and have our being." That spark is not an "it," but rather one spark in the massive energy flow that is eternal, infinite, omnipresent, omnipotent, and which gives us LIFE and makes us LIVE—and while it flows, we ARE BEING itself.

CHAPTER III

Can we define that center? First off, we must ask WHO? "we" refers to in that question. Can homo define man? Can man define God? Or is the correct organization, can God define man (and redefine)? Can man define homo? Do we still have the arrogance to try to command or even grasp God? If that center spark of life is any part of God, then to feel that we (WHO?) are able to grasp IT is arrogance. Look—that spark of life IS US. We do not stand off HERE away from our own BEING and "point back there" (out there) at the spark. If we should ever really become thus separated from that spark, we are DEAD—nonexistent. That is a schizoid response. No, God defines the center, and we CANNOT grasp it or define it. WE ARE IT, and "it" MUST remain unknown to homo. Homo is known, but that "more" which we call "man" is beyond the grasp of homo (and the scientists). We create polarities of concepts (all the time) so that we may distinguish THIS from THAT, man from homo, and then we label the polarities. It is a very useful TOOL, but it is ONLY a tool. It can lead us into believing in the truths of polarity when they are merely constructions of our minds and not truth. We use polarity to distinguish ourselves from others, male from woman, architects from carpenters, etc., but WE ARE NOT THE TOOL. We are sick when we identify with polarities.

So far we have dealt with generalizations. Now we move to be more specific. The conditioning system that we all undergo creates a unique personality in and for each of us, donJuan speaks of this as the "tonal" distinguished from the "nagual." It is homo, but the specific individual—YOU, not the generalization. It is Sam or Wilma: individuals. This entity controls its organism; it identifies with the organism. Then, we feel that we (WHO?) are gods: I, "homo." I AM this organism. "I" control it, and I am aware of no other WAY: ergo, I am the one responsible for the destiny, fate of this organism. Thus, at least for this organism, I am GOD. Then I extend my responsibility to how I effect my environment, thus becoming responsible for my environment and thus how I affect other people. Soon I am responsible for how they respond to me. Thus I become God for myself AND my environment AND the others I contact. Thus it comes about that I, HOMO, AM GOD.

But I, homo, am an animal—destined for the grave and to spend my life sweating to get the money to eat and then shitting and sleeping just so I can do it all over again another day. WHO? can define God? (No—It's "WHO? can define God.") This limited I, homo, cannot be God. I, man, am none of what homo believes. I, man, am more, by definition.

My homo is specific and has a label: a name—the one my culture (parents) gave me. And that name thinks it is alone (solo) in the world. That idea is a necessary part of the process. If it were not solo, it wouldn't be the boss, the commander, the god of and for its own organism. If it were not solo, it would be subject to reality, which it denies in its separate arrogance. Thus scientists insist that there is no more than mere homo in existence. Thus they encourage this arrogant god, commander of the organism.

*

Let us move on to the dichotomy (polarity): order and chaos. Looking at it from the science of physics, chaos is energy moving upon the face of the deep. In chaos, there is only uncertainty, insecurity, and its coordinate fear of extinction: a fall into the abyss. We impose order on chaos because we are then able to cope with it. If NOTHING is predictable, how could we stay out of danger? We create understandable order so that the world will not remain BEYOND our control. The way with which we choose to cope, control, or deal with that chaos is personal to each of us and is done from the very first minute we begin to apprehend that reality: the chaos "out there." It begins when we are yet infants and continues throughout life. There are as many WAYS as there are individuals. But our TRUTH is that there does exist ONEWAY, which clearly incorporates all the other ways.

   That effort to create order out of chaos requires the individual to impose a vast amount of power upon reality. S/he exercises this power in dealing with all hir environment. And, in hir ignorance (arrogance), S/HE CREATES HIRSELF (WHO?) as a specific personality—identity—just for that purpose: of coping and dealing with the chaos-reality and the reality-order around hir AS S/HE DETERMINES IT. And thus s/he creates hir WORLD. That identity is specific to hir world: unique, special, created by homo. Or is it created by God? Or man? WHO?!

WORLD = WEOROLD (Old Eng.) = WERALDH (Teut.)
       = WIROS (man) + ALDH (age): the life and age of man
        WIROS = WIR (VIR) + OS (-AZ: s/he or that which) has WIR

       = WIR = VIR = VIRILE = man, manly, virtue
       = VIS = VITAL, force, vim, vigor, violence
       = VICE = vicious, vitiate; VITU = vituperate: abuse
       = WEI (PIE): to twist
           > wire, thread, wiry, vita, vine, wine (DNA?)
       = WEI (PIE): the vital force that gives
         life, capability of action
THUS WIRAZ: s/he who has the vital force in hir
       = VIRTUE: the having of the vital forces within one
        ALDH = AL + DHE (PIE): to set, put, lay down
           > establish, make happen
       = AL (PIE): to grow, nourish, also high, deep: ALTUS = exALT
         (with the negative AB: AB-AL-ISH = ABOLISH: to
         retard growth)
THUS, ALDH = to establish and actualize nourishment
and thus, growth = OLD, ELDer, ALDerman, adULT
THUS, WIRAZ-ALDH = WER-ALD: the nourishment, growth, maturity, flourishing, and evolution of s/he who has the vital forces within hir.
THUS, WORLD (verb) = to nourish, mature, or lift the vital forces in man to the fullest heights (or depths)
AND WORLD (noun) = the complete history of the nourishment, growth, maturity, flourishing, and evolution of the vital forces in the human, both individually and jointly (how s/he holds to the thread

of life and uses it in action and how s/he learns from hir experience) = not a planet, not material, but the life, experience, and ages of mankind: hir-story.

*

How does that personality—IDENTITY—come about, and why is it so specifically unique? Let us pursue the process step-by-step. It starts back at the time when the individual is but a gleam in hir father's eye. Homo has no control in the choosing of hir parents. How much real control do the parents have? Driven by specifically conditioned likes and dislikes, needs and drives, why these two should couple and make a child becomes a mystery in itself. But they do, and this child is the consequence of their imponderable act. This specific and unique identity, now known as Sam, cannot be responsible for the fact that these two people coupled. It was their choice, but it was affected by cultural drives and meanings hidden deep in their psyches.

We aren't finished yet with that coupling, for we must move to the genetics of the situation. Although these two parents may have been so mature (unlikely) that they are acting out of a clear understanding and noncompulsed choice, yet they have absolutely no control over how the genes line up in matching the two halves that make one individual. Even if the parents choose, through science, some of hir attributes, the child has had no choice in the matter. The result is uniqueness: only the unknown God, if any, has a hand in selecting the specifics of genetic dominance or regression. That is the fate of mankind, for s/he has no hand in the selection process. Through this process of destiny formation, the individual is made and born. Each individual is created by the unknown to fulfill a destiny selected by nature, the unknown—yes, even random chance.

We aren't finished with those parents even yet. For they are the primary conditioning agents for this child. S/he is born nearly a tabula rasa, an empty slate, upon which nurture will write its log. It matters not to decide just how much nature or nurture has to do with the final product, nor to know just how empty that initial slate might be. Both are active here. Each child born into this world finds hirself in a different place from any other child. S/he is born into an environment, milieu—part of this chaotic reality. By their act, these parents have ordained that THIS already-unique child be born into a specific culture, age, and geographic location. The way they raise hir will be specifically culturally conditioned. What was America in 1790 is not America in 1980; New York City is not Montana, and wealthy parents are not poor. Thus family background and expectations, cultural location, period of history all take their toll in marking the individual with additional uniqueness.

Thus, starting from the imponderables of genetics, destiny, or random chance, and moving through the vital and essential conditioning of hir geographical location and the inputs of hir parents through their specific life-styles, psychological problems, and quirks, we arrive at a specifically triply unique individuality whose mix of personality traits are absolutely unique in all of time: never before created, never again to exist. That created by this whole world process is the "son/daughter of man"; and that unique personal identity is given a name by this world—a name that identifies hir as distinguishable from all the others. We must accept this reality—and this TRUTH—and admit that we each carry an identity made by the world, having a convenient label attached: our "given" name. But notice that word: it is NOT "OUR" (possessive) name; it is the one "GIVEN" to us by the world, imposed on us without our will—WILL: that inner center of our being.

*

NAME = NAMA (Old Eng.) = NAMON (Teut)
        = NOMEN (Lat.): name and repute
        = ONOMA (Grk.) also suffixes -onym or -onymy: name
                from GNOSIS = GNOMON = GNO: to know + MON:
                man or individual; THUS, the known one: s/he who is
                named: the named
ALSO an indicator such as the stylus on a sundial
AND one who knows (what time it is), judge, interpreter
        = GIGNOSKEIN (Grk.): intuitive, intellectual, or esoteric
            knowledge; apprehension of spiritual truth
            from GNO (PIE): know, to make known, to declare
        = KEN (Teut.): well-known, usual, familiar = COUTH = KINfolk

= ACCOGNOSCERE = ACOGNITARE = AQUEYNTEN = ACQUAINT

= AD + COM + GNOSCERE: to know completely

= AGNOSTIC = A from AD: not + GNOSTIC: not able to know

= RECOGNIZE = RE: again + COGNOSC-: to know again
> be aware that something has been perceived before

= COGNIZANT: fully informed, conscious knowledge
> CO: intensive + GNOSC-: to become acquainted with

= IN: not + GNORA: know = not know = IGNORE, IGNORANT

= GNOSCERE = NOSCERE = NOTUS = NOTE, NOTICE, NOTION

= CONNOISSEUR: COM + GNOSCERE: s/he knows completely

THUS, KNOW = to become so familiar with something, by careful, attentive, and frequent observation that one may impart it clearly to others.

PLUS MON from ME (PIE): good, timely, seasonal

= MA-TURO = mature, ripe

= MA-NI = MANE, MANUS: God

= MAN, MON: a man, the individual, one = AT-MAN (Sanskrit)

THUS, MON is the good, mature individual,

AND THUS, GNOMEN = NAME: the good mature one who relates clearly and thoroughly about something with which s/he is familiar.

ALSO NAME from NEM: to assign, allot, take

= NIMAN	(Old Eng.)	:	to take, seize
= NAEMEL	"	:	quick to seize = NIMBLE
= NUMOL	"	:	quick at learning
= NEMEIN	(Grk.)	:	to allot
= NOMOS	"	:	portion, usage, custom, law
= NOME	"	:	allotted, pasturage, grazing lot
= NOMAS	"	:	wandering in search of pasturage = NOMAD
= NOM-ESO = NUMES = NUMEROUS (Lat.): number, division NUMBER = an allotted name			

GNO-MON ([g]no-mon) ("n" = nasality on the vowel) = No-Mo, No-Ma, Na-Ma, Na-mo.

Namo (Jap.): meaning (as a verb) "to give homage to, venerate or salute; an exclamation of adoration' from NAMATI (Sanskrit): to bow" = NAME. THUS, "NAME" is a word by which an entity (one: MON) is known—distinguished, valued, represented, renowned (re-known-ed).

We have corrupted the meanings. NEM is the root of NAME only so long as all that is involved is a labeling (assignment) for equal allotment purposes (a number would do). But NAME's root is not NEM, but GNO—to know, understand, and value; its original meaning included the repute, esteem, maturity, and value of the person to which the label pointed.

Thus, NAME is about giving esteem, homage, veneration, and salute to the value, repute, knowledge, maturity of the honored one, by which he is known: the true meaning of NAME. In action: a bow of respect.

Since our given name does not represent anything about who and what we are, it is merely an issued NEM (number) so we can be accounted for by others—those who use it to keep track of their (ownership) serfs.

*

If the reader reviews this process, s/he will note that the individual is not responsible for the making of hir identity. S/he did the job; s/he made it, but as a child, s/he "knew not what s/he was doing." S/he was merely responding to hir milieu (family, etc.) in the best fashion that s/he was able. S/HE IS NOT GUILTY for the product, results, and consequences. The product is produced by this world, hirself, hir parents, hir milieu. They are responsible. OR is it God who created all this? It is a self-made job in response to the chaos as that self (WHO?) sees it. But even that comes about by fate, destiny—God's hand in all of this unknown.

The name that we are given is specific; it refers to that result arising out of the order that was imposed on the vast imponderable chaos of inputs into the makeup of that unique personality: the identity. Thus, we conclude two truths for each person. One, s/he has a specific unique personality (the identity) having a handy label attached for reference to that specific identity. Use of this label-name accesses ALL hir personality, identity, and its history and conditioning (hir WORLD). S/he is the local representative of *Homo sapiens* : the thinking, conditioned determined animal. If s/he believes (loves) hir name, s/he knows that s/he (WHO?) exists because of the reinforcements provided by hir parents and society. Second, there is something else within hir that is indefinable, by definition: the center, which is the local representative of human, Buddha, Christ, God.

We have used the word "center" so far; that point at which the life-force (WIR) enters the organism—the spark of life, unknown, undefined, unapprehended by homo: the place where God enters into homo and creates life. The Kabbalah sets the sixth sephirah (Tipareth) as the center of the Tree of Life where the divine spark enters, creates life—where the king sits on the throne (Mount Meru) surrounded by hir realm or temple (the organism). It is the place where cosmic forces are translated into physical forces, beings, entities, identities—above which mankind (WHO?) cannot reach and below which God cannot effect: the Christ-point where the divinity is sacrificed (transmuted) for humanity and the human (WHO?) is sacrificed for God.

CHAPTER IV

From birth and its initial formation, the identity has been in command of the organism. And in its individuality, it desires to remain in command of itself (WHO?). Thus, it resists strongly any indication that command might be taken away from it. Thus, the identity fights to maintain itself as the center of viability of the organism. Viability, though, clearly lies with the spark of life, which enters in at the center. And the identity denies, as its best defense, the existence of any other possible center. Psychology refers to the ego as the center of command. But "ego" refers only to the psychological self, not the whole of the organism. Here, "identity" points to the whole being: how one walks, stands, the tone and timber of hir voice, whether s/he is aggressive, and the size of hir muscles, as well as whether s/he sees things idealistically, pessimistically, or realistically, hir endurance, and hir stick-to-it-iveness. All these, and more, sum to more than ego. Here we build a concept of the entire living adult individual, including every facet of that being, leaving NOTHING (NO THING) behind, and label it: identity. It is the natural homo, PLUS ALL hir cultural conditioning raised upon hir experience (WER-ALDH): homo and hir world.

*

IDENTITY = IDEM (Lat.): the same + ENTITY (Lat.): that which is true or real; the same or likeness of that which is truly or really in existence. This (identity) is same (identical) with that entity, which is described or pointed to as the reality. Unity and persistence of personality, individuality, condition of being the same with something defined, described, or pointed to as having the character described.

IDEM: pronoun and adjective referring back to the same, itself previously mentioned.

from ID (Lat.): it, the neuter of IS: s/he = I

    I = ISLIK = LIKE; ILCA = ILK: same

      ALSO:IO-N = YON, YONder: THAT (there)

      ITERO: again; IDH: again (anew)

      I-AM = yam, yat, ja, ye, yea, yes: affirmative

      YIET = YET; YIF = if

      ITIUM = ITEM = thus, that

      ID = IDEAL = IDEALIS = IDEA (see infra)

             Existing as a patterning or archetypal idea

Perfection of kind, perfect exemplar of the type or species.

Mental images, conceptions, ideas—standard of perfection.

      = IDIO- (prefix): private, personal, separate, peculiar, distinct.

      = IDIOT: a person of private or common station in life> an uneducated, ignorant, unlearned, or simple person.

      = IDOL = EIDOLON (Grk.) from EIDOS: to see >

          Image, phantom—the form, shape, or figure;

The representation (idea) or symbol of a deity or other being;

Any image or representation of the aspect, likeness, or appearance of something;

That on which the affections are set (including ideas); an object or person greatly loved or devoted to;

Form, image, appearance without substance: phantom;

Pretender, sham, imposter, impersonation (of the real).

      = IDLE = IDEL = IDOLE = IDELE = IDOLUM = EIDOLON;

      = IDEL: void, empty—see IDOL

THUS, vain, mere, empty, no worth, foolish, unemployed.

      = IDYLL: little form or picture

      = EIDULLION diminutive of EIDOS;

IDEA = EIDOS (Grk.): to see > form, picture, model, class, notion; from WEID (see infra);

To visualize or perceive, image, or fantasize an archetype, pattern, or conception—of any perfection—usually restricted to a plan, purpose, intention, or design of action;

The embodying form or exemplar of a conception, person, or thing; a real likeness or representation of a thing;

An embodiment of the essential nature or character of something;

The typical quality that exists in the individual thing and makes it symbolic of analogous things or conceptions (suchness);

A mental transcript, image, picture of an object whether sensible or spiritual (a script); but "the map is not the territory."

Any object of the mind, existing in apprehension, conception, thought, notion, or mental impression (beliefs, illusions, fantasies);

A belief, opinion, doctrine, supposition, or impression;

Plato: species or class name: truth, essence, primordial meaning: suchness.

WEID (PIE): to see (perceive clearly)

    = WITAN (Teut.): to look after, show the way,

        guide, guard, ascribe, or reproach, WIT;

    = WITI = WITE (Old Eng.): fine, penalty (in no wite);

    = WEID-TO = WISSAZ (Teut): the known = WISSEN;

    = WIS (Old Eng.) = WISE; WISEdom

    = GUISE (Frankish)

    = GEWISS (Ger.): certain, sure

    = WEID-OS = WEIDAZ = EIDOS (Grk.): form or shape = IDEA:

        (A [not] + EIDOS = HAIDOS = HADES = the invisible underworld)

    = WID= WIT: knowledge or intelligence

    = WID-E = VID (Lat.) = VIDERE = VISUS: to see or look

    = WID-ESYA = IDEA (Grk.): appearance, form

    = WID-TOR = (w)HIS-TOR (Grk.) = HISTORY: wise, learned

    = WI-NDNO (Celt) clearly visible

        > white (Irish, Welsh)

    = WOIDO = VEDA (Sanskrit): I have seen > I know > knowledge

THUS, WEID > IDEA > IDEM > ID = to see, look at > perception and awareness > the seen, the perceived, the known, the certain, knowledge > wisdom, wise, guide, and learned.

THUS, ID is the form, shape, picture, image, apparition, phantom, appearance, pattern, manner, model, exemplar, class, symbol, representation, belief, opinion, doctrine, supposition, IDEA of that which has been seen, perceived, which follows from the knowledge and the judgment of it.

ID = the form, image, phantom, manner, symbol, belief, idea of that which has been perceived, that SAMENESS and SUCHNESS (except for the weaknesses inherent in mankind's processes of perception) that actually exists.

ENTITY = ENTITE: essence or isness (suchness) = ENTITAS (Lat.)
      = ENS, ENT-: thing, pres. part of ESSE: to be = ES
      The fact of existence or being
      A real being, whether in thought (idea = conception)
      or in fact (being, essence, existence, suchness).

An ID-ENTITY is that form, image, phantom, symbol, belief, or idea of that essence, isness, suchness, existence, being that has been perceived and differs from it according to the limitations of the perceptual apparati.

FINALLY: THIS   (description, model, set of parameters)
    IS THE SAME AS   (equal to, identical with)
    THAT ENTITY   (the being truly
    POINTED TO AS THE REALITY   in existence)
    Y H W H
    I AM THAT I AM   To be distinguished from reification

*

Can we shift command of the organism homo away from the identity; that is, can Sam give up control of hirself? That existing system appears to be exactly what makes hir human, which is the truth: "homo" IS human (see HUMBLE, pg xxx). That control over hirself lies within hirself is also true (location). But s/he sees all of this through the eyes of hir identity (obviously). There can be no other way, for s/he has lived hir years with the identity in command and KNOWS of NOTHING else. Will that identity allow God (fate, destiny, nature, chaos, random chance, NO-THING) to command the organism? No WAY! S/he has spent a lifetime combating that chaos and expending hir power to impose HIR (WHOSE?) order (WAY) on it. Now, after all these years, is s/he to relinquish that? Never!

It is our linguistic trap that lies in the ambiguity of the word "self" (WHO?). So long as "self" is the identity, then identity has NO CHOICE to give up self. But when "self" refers to two DIFFERENT centers, one of them may control the other. In writing, "self" may be capitalized in order to demonstrate which center of organization one intends to refer to: "Self" to the center and "self" to the identity. But try that with the spoken word.

If God were in command of the organism, then what it might create would, of necessity and definition, be the son/daughter of God, not this identity (the son/daughter of man, by definition). So homo defines God, and thereby, God becomes a known—understandable and, thus, predictable. Homo then surrenders to hir defined, thus limited, God who will never get out of hand and lead hir wrong WAYS (according to the gospel of the identity). The identity thus assimilates GOD within itself and continues in command. "Surrender," indeed, becomes rather "domination." The identity, being STRONG enough, has found the way to bring God under ITS control. (See the Beatitude of meekness, page xxx). Remember, God is the invoked, and we all invoke our identity as the need arises. It becomes clear that there is more than one object noun to invoke. And we must begin to awaken to discover just what (WHO?) we invoke.

But it was God who was in command of the world all the while we were maturing our identity. God set up the genes and placed this homo in its specific milieu. Survival through all that chaos occurred because of the fates, not because of the identity's efforts. The identity lives an illusion. It hallucinates that IT is in command, and it is in love (s/he believes) with that illusion: itself, which is narcissism. By definition, illusions are not reality. Reality is OF God; illusions are OF our identity.

And when the identity is confronted with the choice (no, the identity cannot CHOOSE to allow God command over the organism; it is through this process that the identity STAYS IN command) of leaving go of the organism, of getting out of command, of surrendering command of the organism's to another's control, then fear and panic set in. It is an existential problem in which the identity knows only of life (in command) OR death (out of existence). If it is to death AND REBIRTH, that can ONLY mean the end of the identity

27

(death). It is not able to see itself as a mere tool of the organism: its arrogance is too great for that.

The identity was formed by the individual for the purpose of coping with the milieu in which it found itself. For the mature person, life brings changes in its milieu, for which that identity is not suited. The simplest example is marriage (formal or otherwise), wherein two people of differing milieu of backgrounds come to live together. Their identities were formed for service within their own familial milieus. Now they each constitute a new milieu—for each other—totally unlike the old. Their identities cannot cope (by definition). So they must change, adapt. Marriage is thus THE most important growth incentive for the young maturing adult. This kind of intimate and powerful motivation is necessary to provide the opportunity for them to learn about the inherent weaknesses of their OWN identities.

INTIMACY: being INTIMATE = INTIMATUS pp. INTIMARE (Lat.):
to put or bring in, publish, announce, hint;
= INTIMUS: inmost, deepest (-MO: superlative), innermost
EN + TIMERE = to seek or find = EN + TIME' (tim-ay)
EN = most inner; TIME' (Grk.): honor, value, or worth.
THUS, INTIMACY is to be seeking, reaching for, and finding the furthermost inner secret value, worth, treasure in the other.

But people thoroughly conditioned, indoctrinated in their own NOTOKness will resist INTIMACY because they KNOW (are so certain, convinced) that the inner secret is no treasure "of great price," but rather BAD, EVIL—HORROR. Thus, they demand that the surface—so carefully prepared and manicured—be accepted. They resist, refuse, and reject the penetration (yes, the sexual metaphor) necessary for INTIMACY.

*

Assuming that God created animals, how do they respond to a changing environment? Without evolution, they have a problem. First, it is a fact that the environment changes. Over millions of years, any particular environ has changed drastically. An animal that is fixed to eating X (horses eat grass, not mice) will die when its particular food supply is unavailable. If it has no way of changing, adapting to a changing environment, it is doomed to extinction. All life that God/nature has produced would have been extinct as the world changed.

In order for God/nature to keep its production alive, it must provide a way of adaptation. Natural selection is such a way. Each generation is provided with sufficient variety so that some are more able, apt, sure to survive and breed than others—and thus pass on some of the elements of the variation that were successful.

Any generation varies about a mean; thus, there are taller proto-giraffes, and shorter ones. If the environment shifts so that the taller have the advantage, the shorter are weaker, less able to breed successfully, and the taller conversely more able. If these environmental conditions remain, then each succeeding generation of taller giraffes are more successful. There will be fewer and fewer of the ordinary giraffes and more and more tall ones.

Eventually, there will be no more of the original-sized giraffes, and what an observer (if any) would see would be a new species: "Giraffe." This might take one hundred generations, but that can be achieved in a couple centuries or so. With the thousands of years available, evolution by natural selection is no amazing thing.

Consider the tiger and gazelle. The tiger lives by eating gazelles and is the gazelle's worst enemy. But what is it to be a tiger or a gazelle? The gazelle is especially wary and has great speed; the tiger, great stealth and acceleration. How did the gazelle develop what is the essence of gazellity? To stay alive, s/he had to apprehend the tiger and move away before the tiger charged. How did the tiger become so stealthy and able to accelerate? The tiger unable to catch gazelle starves. Thus, it is the gazelle who developed tigerishness in the tiger, and vice versa: the tiger who created the wariness and speed of the gazelle. To be who they are, they need each other. To develop one's self to the height of being requires the other.

Evolution is a God-imposed force that is omnipresent in all our lives, and we respond (there is no choice) to it. The status quo appearing in our lives is our reluctance to allow change. But changing ecology demands that we flow with the flow. And when we do, we are no longer what we were before: the status quo has been defeated. Mankind evolves, like all animals. S/he grows, changes, and becomes something other—both as individual and mankind. It is hir fate and hir beautiful virtue. S/he is not doomed to any single class, caste, status, role, duty, identity; hir destiny is multiplicity. To deny this is to deny the human condition—an exercise in futility. Each of us is born to grow, bloom, flower, fruit into a multitude of forms, experiences, shapes, identities.

And this also applies to dogma. A statement laid down in 1517, restated in 1685, 1787, 1863, 1933, and again today is perforce unchanged. But the environment has undergone vast changes. And so too the psychological loading that people put on the words. Thus, it is a foregone conclusion that the dogma is no longer relevant as stated (it was last fully relevant in 1517). Certainly there is a truth BEHIND, WITHIN that dogma, but the DOGMA, per se, should be discarded for a new restatement of the spirit of the law that fulfills it. And what we mean today is not what was intended by ancient dogmatists.

*

So the identity fights to retain the throne of dominance over its organism. Those words translated into political language symbolize the power and control of a STATUS QUO monarch, who quite naturally resists change: especially the change of monarchs. The identity MUST deny one specific TRUTH of reality: that all living things grow—from infancy to old age until death (horrors!). Life equals growth. The identity insists that its infantile attitudes, sets, and neuroses MUST remain in command of the organism. Thus, the identity must resist growth.

To commit one's self to survival, when death is an absolute, is a losing strategy of unhappiness and neurosis, for one is ultimately doomed to fail to survive. But to accept this obvious truth requires the acceptance that our present identity must be changed ("put away childish things"). And when an organism ceases growing, IT IS DEAD. And so too is ANY status quo organ, organism, monarch, state.

But the threat of losing control to some chaotic unknown is countered with panic (which mobilizes all the defenses); "I can't DOO that!" (WHO?). Of course, the identity cannot. WHO? will be there to reassure the identity? That wail of panic is to be respected (it will probably win the game, anyhow) whether it is a childish scream of anguish, the calm measured terms of rationalization, or a cold analytical statement about lack of skill. Inherent in the set of the identity is the insistence that no other center of organization can be possible. The identity is quite willing to go down to defeat rather than surrender command to another, including fate or God. Witness suicide: the identity, being ignorant of the God within, keeps control to the last and ultimately orders the destruction of the organism before it will ever relinquish control.

What is this panic that the identity exhibits? Is it the fear of death? NO, it is the fear of extinction, which is the fate worse than death (FWTD). The Bible calls it "hell's fire and brimstone." Freud called it the "castration complex," as a way of indicating how terribly frightening it is. It is not a fear of the extinction of the body (witness man's capacity at self-sacrifice). It is the fear that the IDENTITY (that GOD!) will be extinguished. The identity is afraid that it doesn't exist (DOES IT?). That is our FWTD—of which we are all scared out of our skins.

God is also able to organize the being and protect it (by definition). This isn't a belief; this is a definition, a concept, that we set the word "God" (good) to symbolize. The center is the God "within." It is another organizing center, and IT IS ABLE to do the same job that the identity so eagerly insists upon keeping. Will the identity give up command, or will it cling tightly to the throne? Here we have conflict: the identity opposes the Christ-center point of being. The very existence of that organism depends absolutely on that spark of energy (life) flowing from that center point. And yet the identity would deny that (deny the Christ). If it were open-minded, it must SEE the TRUTH: that it DOES NOT energize this organism; it merely uses and directs that energy. It was created by the human (WHO?) to deal with the world in THE WAY nature (God) intended when it placed this uniqueness upon the earth ("IN the world").

The enemy is s/he who would be God: the ego, homo, the identity, the devil. Our present socioeconomic-cultural milieu is dominated by the scientific attitude that places and maintains the identity on its status quo throne and denies the existence of any other WAY. The reinforcements of the scientific attitudes are, in fact, counterproductive of maturity.

Transactional analysis, as founded by Eric Berne and later developed by Claude Steiner, taught us script analysis. These men used the word "script" to indicate a concept similar to "identity." It is far more than mere social roles and is an outgrowth of modern specialization. Job specialization creates roles in society, which demand different aptitudes and skills. A lifetime's practice of such specialized roles creates a personality, a script, an identity that is also specialized to support effectiveness in hir milieu, environment. When one's identity is tied to a specialized role, s/he generalizes hir identity to include that role. S/he then IS a lawyer, doctor, plumber, truck driver. In truth, s/he IS none of these. S/he IS FAR MORE: HUMAN! To free hir from the captivity of hir identity is our intent (the truth shall set ye [WHO?] free). But to do that, first s/he must become aware and then KNOW that another possible center of organization does, in fact, exist.

CHAPTER V

Eric Berne (transactional analysis founder) translated a psychological term into common parlance—that we are either OK or NOT OK: OKness or NOTOKness. He said that we are all born princes (or princesses) and that our culture, society, family, and associations turn us into frogs. WE ARE OK. Contrast this with Christianity's idea of original sin: we are all NOTOK, being sinners ab initio. But there is a semantic problem with the word "original": first, primo, primary, prime, original. There is a difference between the concept of "first," "initial," which determines everything thereafter; and "primary," being MOST important and which affects everything connected with it. The president's wife is the First Lady, but she is not Eve. It is Christianity's CHOICE to make us all NOTOK from the beginning of time without recourse (except, of course, to the church). The fundamental sin of homo is the shift of responsibility for hir behavior away from hirself to "out there." It is what Adam and Eve did when they blamed, respectively, Eve and the snake. That is the first, primary, and most important sin.

Is it true that we are OK? Here is another problem in semantics, not beliefs. What God creates is, by definition, perfect. It is impossible for God to create imperfection. In every case (no matter how imperfect it seems to us), God creates exactly what s/he wants, including the so-called imperfection. Since what s/he wants is "perfection," then "imperfection" IS "perfection"! After all, if God wanted something other than what s/he created, s/he would have created that "other" (unless s/he makes mistakes?). God has created everything, including each imperfect homo. If God had not wanted that specifically designed homo in existence, with its peculiar traits and idiosyncrasies, s/he would have created something different, designed otherwise. God desires what s/he creates. And what God creates is OK (God saw that it was good = the invoked saw that it was fitting—that it fit its place).

But we use "perfect" wrongly; it does NOT mean "without blemish."

PERFECT = PERFECTUS (Lat.), past participle of PERFICERE: to complete = PER: completely + FACERE: to do or make.
THUS, PERFECT is to make completely, finalize, or simply complete; thus, it is whole, nothing to be added—it is finished and completed. God completed a hunchback; thus, s/he is PERFECTED (i.e., God made exactly what s/he wanted). It is only man (homo) who is so limited of view and asleep that s/he judges God so negatively.

Western culture has denied the unity of bad and good through its schizoidness. But facing the truth, if one wishes to build a wooden house (a good), one is forced to cut down trees (a bad). If one wants to discover hir strengths, s/he need only examine hir weaknesses. Yes, one who is a great reader, thinker, analyst, or writer will also tend to be a loner, not communicate hirself to family and friends and not be very enterprising in this world—and may require an aggressive doer for a spouse. But the aggressive doer is a person who does not feel the need to withhold action before thinking: impulsive. Impulsives disrupt an orderly world, but they get things done. So if a person wishes to know hir shortcomings (do I have those?), s/he needs only look at hir strengths and s/he will discover them. It is a human trait to divide good from bad. One person's tragedy may be another's salvation.

Christianity has promulgated the idea of NOTOKness. But it must be excused (we may not allocate guilt if we wish to promulgate OKness). Christianity is no longer the WAY of Jesus, but has, instead, become the cultural religion, which reflects the common consensus of its culture: Western civilization. And guilt is an essential ingredient in Western culture. Thus, these semantic errors are necessary.

*

In our ignorance of what the King James scholars intended with the language of their times (circa 1585), we have imposed our common meanings on the words. But such meanings are culturally conditioned and thus unknown to us since the words are emotionally loaded in the unconscious. And we will remain ignorant of the word meaning until we bring our own personal word-loading up front, where they can be seen. Thus, we must work on our own ignorance of ourselves. For instance:

CHURCH = CHIRCHE (Mid. Eng.) = CIRICE (Old Eng.) (c = k sound)
    = KIRIKA (Teut.) = KURIKON (Late Grk.)
    = KURIAKON (Grk.): that (DOMA understood: house) of the
    Lord
KURIAKOS: of the Lord, from KURIOS: Lord
from KEU (PIE): to swell, or a hole
    = KOU = KAW = CAVUS (Lat.): hollow, CAVE, conCAVE
    = KU = KUMOLO = CUMULUS (Lat.): heap, mass, CUMULATE
    = KURO = swollen, thus strong, powerful
    = KURIOS (Grk.): master, lord, CHURCH, KYRIE, KIRK
THUS hole, hollow, cave, AND to swell, heap, mass, swollen
THUS, to cumulate, be powerful; THUS, master, lord.
THUS, CHURCH is THAT (cavern, house) of the powerful master (of the house) (a continuation of patriarchy: PATRON: PATRE; father, master).
CHURCH was the English word used in translation from the Latin:
ECCLESIA = (Grk.) EKKLESIA: duly summoned assembly
    = EKKALEIN: to call out or summon
    = call someone to come out from hir present place
    = EX: out + KALEIN: to call
     from KEL (PIE) =
    = KLA = HLOW = LOW (as cattle)
    = KLA-MA= CLAMARE (Lat.) = CLAMOR, EXCLAIM
    = KAL = KALA = HALA = HAIL
    = HALEN = HAUL (while chanting)
    = KALYO = CON-CILIUM = CONCILIATE, COUNCIL
    = KALAND = KALENDAE
    = CALENDAR: public announcement of dates
    = KALEYO = KALEIN (Grk.): to call
    = ECCLESIA: called to the side of > to help

> the Comforter: the Holy Ghost.
= KLE = CALARE (Lat.): to CALL
= KLERO = KLARO = CLARUS: bright, CLEAR
= KLE-DHE: to put, place, set down > establish
= KLAD = KLADI = CLASSUS (Lat.); summons
= division of citizens for purposes of the polis
    after summoning them to the place of gathering
= CLASS

ALSO KEL: warm, heat, protected, CALorie, LEE
  : to cover, conceal, save, HELL, HOLE, HALL, conCEAL
  : to drive, set in motion, HOLD, HALT, CELerity
  : to be prominent, HILL (stand out high)

ALSO GHEL: to call = GELL (Teut.): to shout
    = GELLAN (Old Eng.) = YELL; GIELPAN (Old Eng.) = YELP
    = GALAN (Old Eng.) = nightenGALE

AND GHEL: to shine, YELLOW, brightness, GOLD

THUS, call, clamor, hail, chant (while working), shout, yell
> summons, duly summoned assembly, council, conciliate bright,
    clear, shine, yellow, gold
> to be prominent, hill, stand out, shining
> warm, protected, cover, conceal, save, in the lee to drive, set in
    motion, hold, halt

THUS, ECCLESIA = a duly called out (summoned) assembly
(of those who chant, shout while working?)
(no definition of who assembles or who does the calling: God?)
which is: bright and shining clearly
  warm, protective, covered
  prominent, the city (polis) on a hill
but which sets things in motion (the leaven).

THUS, the Greek ECCLESIA is that prominent, clearly shining, summoned assembly of persons, which is warm and protective and which initiates things;

WHILE the Germanic CHURCH (supra) is THAT (cavern, house) of the powerful master (of the house): patriarchy.

What the English meant comes from their feudal culture, CHURCH: the all-powerful Lord orders men to his house away from the rest of the world. We are to depart in peace and thereafter make no waves.

What Jesus intended is clearer from ECCLESIA: God calls men together in a prominent shining assembly both to warm and protect each another and to initiate action in the world. "Where two or three are gathered together in my name." The Amer-Indian uses the SOUTH to symbolize warmth, summer, growing things; thus life, mutual social tribal support, and thus love. When people sit, erect the Shushumna, they shine and become prominent. We are told "Prayer moves mountains." We are to be the leaven, which initiates growth among people.

These two words may properly be distinguished as the Semitic idea of relationship translated into Teutonic terms of power and dominance.

*

All people were born in the Garden of Eden. But there is a basic difference between Eastern and Western religions. Christians behaved so badly in the garden that they were thrown out by God. But people of the Eastern persuasion have never left the garden. They see themselves as still there, dancing in the garden, enjoying its delights, while the Christians are bending and breaking their backs (loaded with guilt) trying to work their way back in. And it was Jesus's message (LOGOS) of the WAY to free us all from guilt.

Guilt is not caused by Christianity or by Western culture. It is indigenous to homo (sapiens), humanity, the organism. Remember how the identity arises in the individual organism. As an infant, child, s/he finds hirself tiny, weak, and powerless to affect hir environment. S/he is terrifyingly dependent on others for hir continued existence. S/he concludes that there must be something wrong with hirSelf. The basic set of NOTOKness requires the continuing imposition of self-discipline to make oneSelf better, thus different, indicating dissatisfaction with the given: that perfection created by God. If s/he is to have the opposite set, OKness, hir parents have their job cut out for them to reinforce that OKness, in the face of the fact that s/he feels and is less than competent to cope with hir environment. The very first requirement for the parents is that they themSelves believe in their OWN OKness. Here we see the power of the culture to further NOTOKness in us all. In nature, a child is raised closely involved in the life and doings of an extended family or tribe. But in Western civilization, the nuclear family is separated from the business life of the world, which reinforces the set of being left behind, lost, alienated—thus NOTOK.

If hir parents treat hir as if s/he were NOTOK, s/he may, in defense, conclude that it is THEY who are NOTOK since there is nothing obviously wrong with hirSelf. Christianity merely supplies the rationalization for this thorough-going set of NOTOKnesses. The church's (one foundation) sin is following the cultural set rather than competing against it.

The very conditioning process that we all undergo, which we all must endure in the very early and tender years, change us from true perfection (OKness) into a horror (NOTOKness). That system convinces us that we ARE NOTOK. And we (WHO?) draw the conclusion, with finality, that it is our fate, duty, to strain, work, perform, and perfect ourSelves (WHO?). Thus we stretch and strain for perfection ("Every day in every way, I get better and better"). Thus optimism is extolled in the service of NOTOKness. But that isn't optimism based on reality, but rather on the illusion—the confident belief in the idea that the world is bad: NOTOK. Contrariwise, the truth is that what God has made; what God has ordained IS GOOD, OK, TRUE, RIGHT, RIGHTEOUS.

The authoritative Christian responds with the aggressive accusation: "Are you trying to be GOD?" "Who do you think you are? GOD?" or "You are the Antichrist."

In the first place, hir accusation may be well-placed since the ego/identity is quite able and willing to take a "Jesus Christ" position in the organism, the zenith of arrogance: the anti-Christ. This is equivalent to being captured, occupied, possessed by a devil OR obsessed, compulsed by an archetype.

But the Christian's objections arise from hir own sense of NOTOKness. S/he cannot (it follows inexorably) accept the possibility of being a god, for that is totally inconsistent with hir NOTOKness. Being addicted to and obsessed by NOTOKness, s/he MUST (s/he is compulsed) fight with all hir possible tools and strength for hir back (negativism and NOTOKness) is to the wall.

So we cannot answer hir accusation directly. If our answer actually communicated successfully, s/he would be destroyed. And conversely, if our answer even appears inept, s/he will destroy us. So we must use the Zen answer, which appears insane (to the common man), instructive (to the student) and correct (to the master): "To WHO? do you address your question?"

Predictably s/he answers: "YOU [you SOB]!" There is no way, at this point, to communicate truth to such vast ignorance. Jesus suggested that it was wheel-spinning to throw "pearls before swine" (truth to those incapable of using such nourishment). Thus, to hir insensitive response, we MUST back off. There is no sense in playing hir game of "Who?"-"You," "WHO?"-"YOU!", etc.

But then, how can we respond to hir answer "you"? Who IS s/he addressing? What s/he sees is what s/he hirself (WHO?) is projecting. In a very real deep sense, what s/he sees (a) does not exist, (b) is a hallucination in hir own mind, and (c) has nothing to do with "you" (since what s/he sees is in no way "you" by any definition). Hir answer concerns the parameters of hir own projection, of which s/he is totally unaware.

So we MUST (are forced by nature) learn to deal or cope with this matter of the projections of others. First, let us distinguish the Messiah complex or that compulsion wherein we MUST cope with the projections of others. We must assess whether we are wasting our time trying to cope with this ignorance. Dealing with this authoritative, aggressive Christian is our CHOICE and should be made according to some purpose, goal, or strategy, and not out of duty. We NEED not respond at all.

So, first, we turn away from the confrontation with another Zen tactic; this one concerning OK- and NOTOK-ness. S/he accused us of trying to be God. We responded, "Who?" and s/he said, "You." And now, meekly, "Oh"; sadly, "I have no feet"; amusedly, "Where are your eyes?"; hurtly, "Don't do that to me!"; simply, shake your coat or finger at hir silently and walk away; or just stand there and say nothing at all ("Don't just do something, STAND THERE!"). But never project NOTOKness upon hir. "LOVE YER ENEMY."

Whatever else hir projection, s/he is projecting NOTOKness on US. Do WE BECOME NOTOK because of hir projection? Why do we think s/he can MAKE us NOTOK? It is an infantile belief that stems from our dependence on parents. In fact, they can not only make us NOTOK, they can injure, maim, or destroy us. That s/he is authoritative does not make hir our parent, nor us hir dependent child; s/he is not actually injuring us. But, of course, s/he has arrogated to hirself the role of our parent: s/he acts AS IF s/he were my authority (my father). It is the patriarchal stance by which s/he becomes superior to me, thus manufacturing a defense against hir firm belief in hir own inferiority.

Politically, we are not able to be independent collectively, for we are not independent economically. And such political and economic independence cannot be achieved until we are first independent psychologically. That awaits our shift from infantile dependencies to becoming adult—"man" instead of "homo"—putting aside childish ways and accepting thoroughly that we are OK: made so by God. So we shift our dependence away from this world to dependence on God (the Zen master depends on NO-THING, ever), not a patriarchal God (Jehovah) but the God brought by the Christ (center): love.

*

NEITHER THIS NOR THAT

	(distinguish)		(thing	)	
How do we	(identify)	one	(item	)	from another?
	(specify)		(person	)	
	(personality)				

(A) We do the "THIS/THAT" thing.   *(B)* We give IT a name.

BUT, FIRST, we separate it out from the others: CLASSIFICATION.

HORSE:	larger	DOG:	smaller
	long legs		hairy
	big head		tongue
	hooves		teeth
	mane		paws

OK, so now apply this to Self: We distinguish ourSelves from all others by separating ourSelves from them. We do this by creating our specific IDENTITY.

When is a baby OTHER than its mother?
When is a son/daughter OTHER than hir father?

(decide   )
When one or both (choose   )
(conclude)

The one acts

and the other may accept the attribution.

We try to be distinguishable
by making ourSelves different from/than the others
—and become alienated; thereby,
the greater the difference, the greater the alienation.

When the father insists upon separation,
the son/daughter concludes NOTOKness because of the rejection.

We are not different from or separate. We just imagine the difference.
<<<image, see page xxx >>>

We are compelled to accept the difference by the power (conditioning reinforcements) of parent and society (the common consensus). Then we internalize it and finally believe it ourselves. If we cease distinguishing our identifiable personality (identity),

we become one with them.   We recognize that we ARE them.

Then THIS/THAT is no longer distinguishable.

When we have distinguished ourSelves from the OTHERS
and thus created our IDENTITY;
we find that it is a negative process:

THEY ARE NOTUS, and we are NOTTHEM = each is NOTOTHER.

This is parallel to NOTOKness:

THEY are   NOT (OK)   WE are NOT (OK   )
            NOT (US)   I am   NOT (THEM).

WE   (ALL   ) are NOT (OK   )
        (EACH)   NOT (the OTHER).

As long as I am distinguishable from THEM, then
         either they are OTHER THAN ME and thus NOTOK,
          OR I am OTHER THAN THEM and thus NOTOK.

   If I am indistinguishable,   I MUST BE THE SAME.

Since I am no better or worse than they—thus being same and indistinguishable—THERE CAN BE NO OK OR NOTOK.

*

PREDESTINATION = PRAE (Lat.): before, in front of
    from PER (PIE): in front of, before, forward, through,
        thorough, toward, against, near to, early, first
+ DESTINARE (Lat.): to determine
    from DESTINE: make firm, determine, establish
        from DE (Lat.): down, firmly
+ STA (PIE): to stand (erect), placed, standing
THUS, DESTINE = place firmly in position = determine, establish.
THUS, to PREDESTINE is to establish, make firm and determine that which is directly in front of one: hir path; hir pathWAY: it is a commitment to a WAY.

   "Predestination" is true—or not—depending on what one means when s/he uses the word. The word is merely a label, a pointer that points to some singular concept distinguishable from other concepts. So we might challenge with the question, "Just WHAT is IT that is predestined?"

The scriptures say that it is our WAY, which is set for us by God. But "WAY" is ambivalent; it has more than one definition. Naturally, "way" indicates "path," "road," "route," "career," THUS our future "course" or the "road of life," which lies before us. This is the usual concept that we argue is (or is not) predestined by the fates. Since man has free will and since our own experience shows that we are able to affect the lives of others, we tend to disbelieve in predestination.

We are correct, but we have thrown the baby out with the bath water. "WAY" has another meaning: "method," "process" (the way we do), "manner," "condition," "mode of living." It is place or path but not geographically rather psychologically—not external but internal. Here we are not talking about a future event predestined, but a behaviorism habitually practiced until it becomes predictable: THUS, seemingly by the fates predestined.

Second Samuel 22:33 states, "God... maketh my way perfect."
"Perfect" = PER: thoroughly + FACIO, FACERE: made
THUS, PERFECT = thoroughly or completely made
> completed or finished.
THUS, God has (past tense) completed my WAY.

This does NOT refer to the predestination of one's future route or career, the events that will occur, including death. But this DOES refer to the predestination of one's mode of living, manner of behavior, habits, and conditioned responses. This tells us that it is GOD who has MADE COMPLETELY one's personality—identity.

The center (Christ, God within), awakening in the infant to the world, absorbs the inputs of hir particular specific peculiar environment and, by the age of seven, has completed the erection of that identity, which s/he uses to cope with hir specific environment. S/he is forced to build that temple while still an innocent child, unaware that the world environment is not the same as hir own familial environment. S/he is absolved of the guilt when s/he discovers that that completed self is not relevant in later ages (and new environments). That identity predestines us to behave in predictable ways. It is our compulsions, obsessions, and fears that make this true.

Can we (WHO?) change this? By definition (God made), NO. The problem is WHO? is in command. The alternatives for command are the identity or God, illusion or truth, fantasy or reality.

CHAPTER VI

So the Lord God set up the garden and placed hir two "children" therein. But s/he deliberately provided the two trees, stating categorically that the tree of the knowledge of good and evil, right and wrong, was forbidden to them. They disobeyed that commandment at the instigation of the serpent and were punished for it.

But several things become obvious as prerequisites to this scenario. One, according to the story, the "children" were unable to distinguish right from wrong, good from evil, until AFTER THEY HAD eaten of the tree. In order for the prohibition to be effective, they must already have had the capacity of choice in order to create the possibility of disobedience. If they already had such capability, eating of the tree of knowledge would not have given them anything new. If they did not have that knowledge of right and wrong previous to eating of that tree, they did not have the ability to distinguish obedience from disobedience. Thus being innocent, eating would have been no crime (culpability enters only with the capacity to do wrong), and punishment would have been irrelevant (or beastly, coming from a savage Judge/Lord/God absolutely without compassion).

We can assume that this scenario was not set up by God accidentally: S/he knew what s/he was doing. Accepting the givens inherent in the play, there was only two possible choices: obedience or disobedience. The "children" did not disobey immediately; that came later. But that makes us aware of the interval between the institution of the setting and the act of disobedience. How long did that last? And then we find the second inherent parameter to the scenario: it was posited outside of time. The "children" did not have a sense of time: life was timeless. Time passes only as one can distinguish events, when one has the knowledge of duality: right and wrong, good and evil. Without being able to distinguish night from day, consciousness of the difference does not exist. In fact, the residence of the "children" in the garden is eternal: Paradise and Eden are eternal. The fall of the "children" is the fall into time. The previous interval is, in fact, no interval, for neither God nor the "children" were bound to the limitations of time.

Did God intend that the "children" disobey? Disobedience is negative. God's way is positive. Although eating is a positive act, disobedience is negative. Any day, the "children" might have stumbled accidentally. Where were the rewards (positive reinforcements) for not stumbling? There were none.

Each day that the "children" continued to refrain from eating of that tree was a day of obedience. Thus that obedience was eternal until the disobedience occurs. The "children," in fact, obeyed for eternity (millions of years, perhaps trillions of Kalpas, each equal to billions of years). Finally, ultimately, there was that one act of disobedience that, by itself, ended all that eternal nothing of the garden and commenced the life of mankind as we know it. Without that act, there never would have been humans living on earth in time.

The Lord God set up this scenario to test hir new "children" (yet how "new" after an eternity in the garden?). But did s/he hope, desire, want them to disobey or obey? If s/he wanted them to obey, s/he needed to give them the capacity to distinguish obedience from disobedience, the capacity to know right from wrong, good from evil. And this s/he reserved from them in the forbidden tree. The only other alternative: s/he wanted disobedience (or s/he didn't care: indifference is a value, or non-value, we do not infer in a god; for, by definition, gods always take care of their people).

Thus, we must accept that God set up this scenario with the purpose in mind that the "children" would ultimately get around to disobedience. This in itself supposes evolution if only because they would get bored with an eternity without event of any kind. God could hope that mankind would finally cast around for something exciting to do. So, God provided the snake.

Now that the human had acted on hir own (right or wrong), God MUST (?) respond. Can humanity then force God to a response?

Does God have choice? The story says that God, recognizing that the humans now are like a god, s/he MUST remove them away from the other tree, LEST they gain eternal life too. Thus indicates that God had been deprived of choice. Is our god so limited?

It also says that God chose to keep that tree away from mankind. Was s/he being self-protective, or had this already been planned? If God is omniscient, s/he was not surprised by the act of hir "children; s/he was ready for this scenario an eternity previously. The "children" were already living an eternal life—what need had they for the second tree?

So God set up the whole thing as a necessary part in the development—growth—of mankind. You will not forget that s/he did provide a way back to Paradise. But that entails CHOICE in human hands. God gave mankind free WILL—CHOICE. There are ALWAYS CONSEQUENCES of choice-made, not always good, pleasant, wise, or beneficial to one's self or to others.

But choice in the individual presupposes choice in all mankind. People do, in fact, make their own history. The multitude of choices made by each of us (cigarettes, miniskirts, marriage, TV programs, McDonald's, how we respond to others) are part of the choices made by the society and the peoples of the world. The ultimate consequences of all those choices determine mankind's direction through time: evolution. We are EACH responsible, and our choices are small and insignificant ONLY because we think that way. But we have been given the power to create significant consequences with our power of choice and action. That essential power—what it is to be human—came to us through the scenario provided by God and the act of the children.

*

Let us step back to the Garden of Eden and that original sin story. Read it yourself and find that the punishment (being cast out of Paradise) was not for eating the apple, but for shifting the blame from Self to the other. Adam said, "She made me dooit !"; and Eve said, "Blame the snake!" These are clear shifts of responsibility away from Self to some externality. But again, we have a semantic problem: this time it is the word "responsibility." What does it mean?

46

It is made up of two parts: response- and -ibility, or ability—response ability or the ability to respond. What does that mean to us? To have response-ability means to have sufficient control over our responses that we may choose any specific response we desire to exercise. We have the ability of choosing among several responses to a stimuli in our environment. That ability comes as standard equipment of the organism.

The perfect example is "S/he makes me mad." This refers to some external behavior of another that is, let's say, frustrating. What is our response to that externality? We get (notice the choice of word) mad, angry. But IT IS NOT TRUE that S/HE MAKES ME mad or that we get mad. The truth is that we CHOOSE "mad" as our response. Then we shift the blame for that response away from ourselves to the stimulating other. It is then HIR FAULT, GUILT, for OUR behavior. That is the FIRST SIN, the shift of response-ability to "out there"; the sin that DRIVES (not "drove") us out of Eden—the refusal to TAKE our responsibility. And we do this because we are so convinced of our own guilt that we must shift that burden away from ourselves (projection).

Is homo determined by the stimuli of hir environment? Does s/he have choice in the matter? If a person is walking along a mountain trail and, suddenly, with hir next step, finds an abyss before hir, will s/he take that step? It is hir free choice, given the alternatives, not to step. Which is the truth: determination or free will? BOTH! It depends on which side of the coin you WISH to consider or emphasize: man or homo.

Does our responder have the choice NOT to get mad? If s/he is homo, then, by definition, s/he is determined—s/he has no choice—and s/he makes no choice, even as s/he CHOOSES to shift the blame "out there." That is the way s/he has been conditioned. Can s/he change to another WAY? If s/he is man, then, by definition, s/he has free will and has the ability to choose hir responses. If, in hir ignorance, s/he does not know that there is a conceptual difference, then s/he is lost (and needs to be "saved").

The question is not then the duty to choose or to make a choice. The question is WHO? does the choosing. S/he says, "I can't do that." WHO? "I am able to choose my own responses." Such an independent stance! WHO? is the "I" who thinks s/he can choose hir own responses? For homo, that utterance is pure arrogance. For man, it is the simple truth.

We can (and do) try to perfect our little childish god: our identity who commands this organism. We study, train, and work to improve our(Selves) ability to select alternate responses, but it is a losing strategy. The identity is, by definition, always limited. And it is limited because it was created by a little child (before age 8) who was confused and bewildered by a chaotic morass of indecipherable stimuli all telling hir that s/he was NOTOK. Starting with (sand) a lump of plain rock and polishing, polishing, and polishing for many years will never make a gem out of it, no matter how long, or how hard, we go at it (it may, however, mirror a vague reflection, like the moon reflects the sun, the image and likeness of the truth). The identity is NOT GOD. The identity is only NOTOK insofar that we have inculcated it with our philosophy of NOTOKness. It is the identity that believes in its own NOTOKness—BY CHOICE.

It is God's WILL that we can choose from an infinite set of responses. That is true, once again, by definition. God creates perfection only, and free will is inherent in that completeness. Such choices are made as an ACT of WILL by the Christ-center within us: that God-energy flowing in and through us.

How is response-ability done? By the choice of the individual. And how is that done? Response-ability cannot be given by another, whether s/he be parent, guru, saint, teacher, God, or cop. As you were told a thousand times by your parents, "YOU MUST TAKE responsibility." Catch that word "take"; it indicates the exercise of power: the power that your life has over your life. The parents may have meant duty and, therefore, guilt by their word "responsibility," but that sentence points to POWER when read "response-ABLE." No one can give another the ability to choose responses. Even if one requires advice or permission from some authority, it is still hir own power that s/he exercises. It is the power of command over hir own organism—that power granted by God. To shift command away (the first sin) is to make another into the God who commands ("S/HE makes me mad").

"Original sin" is the label on that ideology that arrogates power to the authoritative speaker and denies it to the listener-subordinate. The true meaning of responsibility empowers the listener ("The truth shall set ye free"). Knowing that you already HAVE the power to choose among responses gives you many more opportunities to choose freedom over slavery: that ancient slavery of NO CHOICE. "Rise up from your bed and walk."

This is the essence of the priesthood (preacher): the teacher has the truth and the power to transfer it to the listener, which changes hir. But Jesus: it is the truth (the ideas) that frees only when you grasp and accept them. That can't be done for you (i.e., the priest doesn't have that power).

Jesus said, "Love your enemies" (Matthew 5:43). Why mention it here? The aware person will immediately imagine a confrontation episode with hir enemy: a purse snatcher approaches. Why is s/he—or how does it happen that s/he is—an enemy? That is, HOW = through what process does this individual become an enemy? It occurs by the choice of the assailant. It is s/he who decides that s/he will make the attack. As s/he approaches, s/he could be a friend, but by hir own selection, s/he makes hirself an enemy. The fact, or conclusion, that s/he is an enemy, and you the victim, is made FOR YOU by this opponent. MUST YOU AGREE with hir? Does s/he have the power to determine YOUR conclusions (what goes on in your head) for you?

If we respond to hir as an enemy, then we communicate that we are willing to dance hir dance of aggression with hir—join hir by playing a role (victim) in hir game of purse- snatching. Are you hir slave? If we have true response-ability, we do not follow hir lead (as to who our enemies are). We can decide that s/he is a friend, a comrade, a buddy (conscious choice, not unconscious reflex). Then s/he has the choice to join us in OUR dance. Hopefully, we offer a more beautiful, more pleasurable dance than s/he did. And in this waltz, we will love hir, the martial art aichito advocates always choosing to serve the assailant's purpose as thoroughly as possible.

If you find such a one within reach and the correct response is to punch hir in the nose, you have a difficult problem. When the moment occurred that the punch was to have been thrown, of necessity, you were thinking and concluding about what was the correct response. And you were NOT throwing punches. Now, seconds later, there is NO WAY to throw that punch BACK THEN. Your punch now will be those same seconds late. Does it matter? YES! What was going through hir mind THEN, if the punch connected, is not what is happening internally NOW. The ordinary flow of consciousness connects ideas and events together; thus, the meaning of that punch to hir varies dependent upon hir inner mental construct. If the punch was correct then, it was because of the flow of ideation moving from the moment though the jarring of the punch to a response. That flow seconds ago is always distinguishable from the flow now occurring. They are two different happenings.

But in making the calculation, can we know what is going on internally in the other's mind as we act? NO, by definition, it is only God, Christ, Center that can know the correct response and timing. Homo can never know what is correct. Only when God (Christ-center) acts in "man" (the act of will) can it be so spontaneous that the punch is never late. This requires being centered.

*

If the ego is stilled (killed), then it is unable to do anything; it actuates nothing. It cannot act, perceive, think, analyze, or conclude. That is, (1) passivity and (2) relaxation.

If SHAKTI, the goddess within, tells me to be passive and accept her love, she means me, the ego/identity. If when centering (meditating), I relax the muscles in my face, the conditioned identity, which gives my face that certain tension known as Sam, drops off. So the four concepts (meditation, centering, relaxation, passivity) are identical, synonymous.

But I fear this: I feel that I have some DUTY to keep the tension up. My parents (and other associates) will be confused if I cease being Sam for them. I have been conditioned to produce Sam at all times (isn't there a law against name-changing?). So that the authorities can manipulate me, they trained me to respond predictably correctly, as they (parents and society) defined it. There never was any choice about it on my part. They named me and conditioned me when I was dependent and vulnerable. And I fear that force, which is always present to ensure that I will be responsive to them when necessary— defined as—whenever they demand.

CHAPTER VII

All this may be every convincing, but the reader will certainly feel the cry of all people (WHO? identities?): How do we get to KNOW the truth? Although that is the human despair of living in chaos and confusion, it has in it the seed of THEWAY. The word "how" points to the fact that we are vitally interested in the PROCESS by which truth can be apprehended. If we unload all the emotional pain and anguish from that question, we find the right question: BY WHAT PROCESS does MANkind get to know the truth? And the answer becomes simple and obvious.

All humanity has but ONEWAY of discovering the truth about existence, life, the world (wer-aldh), the environment, reality. It is by observation, analysis of those observations, setting up tentative hypotheses from the analysis, testing the hypotheses, and finally drawing conclusions about the validity of each hypothesis—all taken from the reality: the environment about us. But it starts with and depends on OBSERVATION: seeing, being awake, watching, perception.

It is a never-ending process, for mankind's mind is limited. When s/he ultimately draws a correct conclusion, that fantastic high, known as enlightenment, or the "aha" phenomena occurs. But just as soon as s/he has grasped THAT truth, new observations begin to make hir uncertain about that conclusion. S/he may elect (yes, choose!) to live in uncertainty, have faith, and suppress hir observations (doubts); or s/he may continue to struggle with the world, that is, to grow.

And in the process, s/he will find that s/he must either choose this personal inner "aha" process or the external status quo (hir own and/ or society's) for the placement of hir loyalty. This latter will stifle hir no matter the rewards granted by the patriarchal dogmatists.

THIS then is the path: THEWAY (Gaté) leading to the continuous finding of new and greater truths about reality: truth that does not falsify the old, but which supersedes it with a greater validity ("I am not come to destroy [the law], but to fulfill [it]").

Does God speak directly to man/woman (homo) or through a book (Bible)? The answer MUST BE "DIRECTLY." Meaning is a process that goes on only in the mind of the observer. The LOGOS is heard WITHIN. The meaning of words is communicated only to one who knows from hir own personal experience what a specific word-label refers to. If the reader's own experience is so limited that s/he cannot distinguish honesty from other alternatives, no articulation can teach hir. But it is when s/he finds a meaningful interpretation of what s/he has already experienced that s/he finds enlightenment in a scripture (merely a writing). But the PROCESS moves FROM what God has already given hir TO the words, not vice versa. God speaks to all directly, constantly, although they may not realize it until they are REFERRED later to a scripture. The person who spends all (or most) of hir psychic energy studying and arguing about the truths to be found in a book is like the s/he who has climbed up a signpost in order to find the WAY. The signboard is necessary and valuable, but the one up the post is NOT ON the path; s/he can only point to it from up there. In order to be on the path, s/he will have to come down from hir ivory tower and put hir feet in THEWAY and get them dirty. Zen: we must never confuse the pointing finger with the moon.

All humans are put on this earth, say the Amer-Indians, as a perceiver, to see and understand this fantastic gift—the earth and everything on it. "A man sits in the Lodge of his Being, Looking out to the East for the 'Enlightenment' to arise 'out there.' If he were Smart, he would lift the Rock of his Law from off the Skins of his Lodge and Look out upon the Prairie in other Directions" (Goes Beyond).

This process for the novice may be an end, which s/he worships. For the master, it is THEWAY of life; s/he continually enjoys—partakes of—enlightenment and its coordinate continual highs: bliss. Instead of enlightenment being a sometime thing and darkness the way of hir life, he makes enlightenment THEWAY and darkness only occurs when hir poor, little, confused, and frightened identity insists on order and certainty ("Fear not!").

The point of this discussion is, which WAY do YOU choose? Zen has another little phrase used to challenge the identity with THEWAY. It is the command: "WATCH IT!" Watch what? Or is it watch who? Or watch WHO?

WATCH: watchful, to watch, to look at or observe attentively and carefully; to look and wait expectantly in anticipation; to watch for opportunity, alert and vigilant; to tend: watch over flocks

= WAECCHEN (Mid. Eng.): to be or stay awake, keep vigil

= WACHTEN (Old Eng.) = WAKTON = WAKAN = WACAN, WACIEN

= WOG: to WAKE, rise and be watchful or watch for, to be brought into a state of awareness, alertness from WEG (VEG, VAK): to be lively or strong

= WOGE (Teut.) = WAKEN, WAKNAN = WACAN, WAECNIAN (Old Eng.)

= WAKE, WAKEN: to wake up, arise and be awake

= WAKJAN (Teut.) = WAECCAN (Old Eng.): to be awake and watch

= WAHT (Teut.) = WAHTON (Frankish): to watch for—WAIT

= WACHTEN (Mid. Dutch): to watch for—guard

= WEGE = VEG, VIG (Lat.)

= VEGERE, VIGERE: to be lively and strong, VIGOR

= VEGELI = VIGIL (Lat.): watchful, awake, VIGILant

= WEGSLO = VELOX (Lat.): fast, lively, speed, VELOCity

THUS, WATCH = to bring to a full state of life, liveliness, awareness, and watchfulness. The Zen masters have said that we are asleep and ought to be awake. They are indicating two things: one, that we must be aroused, kicked into life; and, two, that to be awake is to be alert, aware, and attentive.

It means to be all there—with full attention, here and now, on THEWAY, on the way of your identity, on the center, and on the world (wer-aldh) "out there." See it ALL happening and relating together. In order to draw hypotheses, one must observe data. If s/he is asleep, hir eyes are closed. So Zen indicates that one must be awake and pay attention in order to make the necessary observations. Eventually, one is always awake, making observations, building new hypotheses, and having continual enlightenments, which is now THEWAY of life (PARA SAN Gaté).

All the religions have used their own specific metaphors for all this. They suggest that there is a clear and unambiguous distinction between sleeping and waking states of consciousness. They ask their listeners to use that distinction metaphorically and apply it to the difference between the ordinary waking state of consciousness and the state of (nonordinary) spiritual (mystical) awareness. And the teacher prods us to "WAKE UP"! We are as if asleep as we go about our (WHO?) daily lives. We are unaware of how very much excitement, joy, and bliss there is all around us. A great old Protestant hymn called "WACHET AUF!" is WAKE UP!

Man's consciousness gives him a tool: ATTENTION = ATTEND = AD: toward + TENDERE (Lat.): to stretch = to stretch toward
ATTENTIVE: attending, concentrated, observant, listening
ATTEND: to stretch toward, direct attention to, be present
     : have one's attention in command and directed toward
TEND: short for attend
TENDERE = to stretch out or direct one's course
THUS TENDERE is to move in a certain direction which one is inclined (stretched out) or disposed toward

from TEN = TENERE: hold, keep
    = TENACIOUS: to cause to stretch out, endure, or hold on
    = POR-TEND = to stretch out before
    = TANTRA: he stretches out or weaves
    = TENERO: TENDON, string, THUS delicate and TENDER
Nurses TEND by directing attention in a disciplined, unwavering, continued concentration toward its object.

INTENT = to have in mind, plan, or to mean
    from IN: inner + TENERE: to stretch out
    = hold to one's (inner) course.
THUS to direct and stretch out one's inner (mind) toward something.

THUS, TEND = to stretch out or direct one's mind, having under command one's capacity of observation (nondistracted by nonessentials) or having one's dispositions in conscious control—a firm, enduring, unwavering, impeccable hold on such capabilities; + AD-: to or toward = ATTEND: the directing of TEND toward some object.

It's hard to describe in modern terms what "stretch out" means. If one mimics the action described, one will feel the apprehensive, anticipatory tension that floods the body. Stretching the Shushumna vertically (hanging one's chin on a skyhook) is part of it. This is the feeling that comes when one is truly attentive—centered.

If we pray to God, we ought to attend upon hir, waiting in the humble pose of a servant or supplicant. If you really believe that God will answer you, then you ought to be prepared to catch the answer. PAY ATTENTION, sit UP (yes, under tension) and WATCH for IT like a hawk, for that answer may "come like a thief in the night." STAY AWAKE! "Stretch out" in expectation of grasping what IS arriving. YOU have the response-ability to direct and COMMAND your attention wherever you choose (and it's your choice to be asleep). Now WATCH IT!—PAY ATTENTION!

We have to WATCH ourselves "in here" and the world "out there" at the same time. Where IS the dividing line between them? "Out there" is our environment. But if "in here" is the Christ-center, then "out there" INCLUDES THIS ORGANISM as part of the environment. That means that our identity is part and parcel of the environment: the "out there" world. On the other hand, God is IN the world and all nature is part of God. Then the God "within" means that the "out there" must needs be "in here" also, and at the same time.

The question "Why should we 'WATCH IT!'?" means "What purpose is there in asking, observing, drawing conclusions?" That sentence demands the challenge of "WHO? asks?"—WATCH IT! You were earlier asking for truth.

*

"Ego [identity] IS our attention. Only through the [diversions] that threaten our attention, do we discover interiority. To become [what we really are], requires total freedom of attention. Meditation exercises are helpful. Pure attention is beyond our bodies [WHO?].

When attention acts, duality merges into oneness. There is no room for guilt then. But guilt is useful to put ourselves [WHO?] into question and recall us to the present [which is] being attentive."

In this view, attention (as a label) is equated with the center and with the pure energy flow that Assagioli called "will." Thus this view suggests that our attention is not directed by us but by the center—at least that which was called pure attention. He points out that due to our conditioning, our set for indulgence and our compulsions, addictions, and obsessions (all including guilt), we are distracted from the truth. But that it is through these distractions (if we watch) that we achieve the sought-after unity, enlightenment. As in all things, we get out that equivalence of what we put in (reap what we sow); we obtain as much enlightenment as we put time, effort, and energy into the search.

Attention then is the moving and acting cosmic energy flowing through us, but we allow it to be diverted, stopped, and dammed (damned) by the external distractions in our environment and our lives. And when that cosmic force captures our attention, and we are firmly attentive and attend completely to something, then all duality vanishes for

A. we are no longer body, mind and spirit, but a unified whole;
B. we are so one with the object of our attention that THAT and THIS become one; and
C. so long as our attention does not waver, we are unified with GOD, and then WE ARE GOD.

Our intellect is occupied by the object of our attention, and during this moment (this NOWness), we cannot KNOW the loss of duality and the presence of unity with God. This because REFLECTION (What WAS that? What just happened?) is required in order to KNOW; WE (here) must look at THAT (there), impose the necessary duality and its coordinate separation (and alienation) in order TO know. Unity—God—merely IS. It is after the moment passes that we have the time to reflect and thus to know. We can only know after the fact.

But WHO? is the "WE" in that last? It is our ego/identity, the false little self that we love so much. And ego IS our attention? Yes, the ego/identity/self does not actually exist as a thing. It is a construct that exists only through the power of our attention—in this case, our belief. Thus the major diversion, damming (damning) in our lives is our own ego: the illusory construct upon which our attention is so riveted. And it is only through living in the midst of ourselves that we can discover interiority, what is really there: our attention flowing—an energy flows within which we LIVE, MOVE, and HAVE OUR BEING.

This then is the essence of self-centeredness, self-consciousness, self-interest, selfishness: that the center has the attention of the organism's mind focused on the existence of this false construction of the mind. We (our centers) are distracted to and by this all-important diversion and away from God, truth, life, purpose, living fully and abundantly as we were created for. We must KILL that false construct, concept of individuated Selfness (die to self) and allow the center to have freedom instead of addiction, obsession, compulsion with self. Sri Ramana Maharshi states, "Only the ego is bound by destiny, not the self—and the ego is nonexistent."

*

As this organism grows from its birth throughout its life, it apprehends its environment, the world "out there" through a process best called exploration. Simply put: if the organism were a passive, unmoving (determined) object (an observation platform), the environment available to it would be extremely limited. So limited that only one side of objects would be visible. But THIS organism is designed to enter INto that environment in order to see all sides of a thing (including concepts), to feel, handle, pick up (and drop) things. That exploration process, however, affects the environment and changes it (even our exhalations change the world). Thus we do not explore a thing (stability), but we always explore a happening, for it is continually changing just because WE (individually) are IN it. Thus the environment or world or realty is, in fact, a kaleidoscope. Once more we see energy (WHO?) moving across the face of the deep, continually modifying the scene. At best, we are forever merely apprehending only one specific frame in a moving picture.

But note that we, the identity, the organism, being supposedly adapted to the environment, is faced with something different at all times. It is forced to adapt itself to a continually new environment.

Thus we can NEVER be stable. The identity or organism (they are not the same) is modified BY the environment as it in turn modifies the environment. Stability is thus an illusion obtained by the identity by selectively ignoring certain TRUTHS: part of the reality out there. That is its CHOICE and its way of life.

To be moving out, exploring (Gaté) into the changing flux through this continually changing and unknown world to meet an inevitable destiny or fate is the same as being on a track, trail, path, or WAY. One MUST do this for this is what man is and does—flow with the flow. Now, why cry about such a reality? WHY? Why cry about reality? We cry because this is the WAY the identity discovers that s/he is not GOD, to hir terrible disappointment.

EXPERIENCE: to participate in or partake of personally, undergo
EXPERI-ENCE = -ENS (Lat.): indicates action,
state, quality, or condition
    = EXPERI-ENS (Lat.) presp. of EXPERIRI: to try, test = PER
       THUS EXPERIENCE: the quality, state, act, or condition
      of testing, trying
EXPERT = EXPERTUS (Lat.) = past p. of EXPERIRI = PER
EXPERIMENT = EXPERIRI + -MENTUM
    = -MENTUM (Lat.): indicates product, means, action, or state
EXPERI-MENTUM: the product of an attempt, trial
the means of making an attempt, trial
the act or status of attempting, trial
PER (PIE): forward, through, in front of, before, early, first,
chief, toward, near, against, around, at
    to lead, pass over > cross, FORD, FERRY,
FUHRER (Ger.), journey, PORT, gate, carry
    grant, allot, assign, produce
    = PARARE (Lat.): to try to get, prePARE, equip
    = PARERE, PARIRE (Lat.): to get, beget, give birth = PARENT
    = PAROS: PAR: begets, produces + OS: AZ: s/he who produces
    = PAUPAROS: producing little > poor = PAUPER
    = PARIKA = PARCAE (Lat.): the fates who assign destiny
      > to lead over, press forward, be first > to try, risk
    = PERAZ = PER + AZ: s/he who or that which
    = FERAZ (Teut.): danger: FAER (OE): sudden calamity: FEAR

= PERICULUM (Lat.): trial, danger > PERIL

= PERYA = PEIRA (Grk): trial, attempt, experiment = PIRATE
   EMPIRIC < EMPEIRIKOS (Grk.) = EMPEIRA: experience

= EMPEIROS: experienced in (EM = EN: in)

= EX-PERYO = EXPERIRI: to try, learn by trying

= EX: out of, away from, outward + PERIRE

= PER + IRE: to go = EI (PIE)

= PER-IRE: to go forward, press forward

= EX-PERIRE: To press forward, lead, go first, on the path, journey—away from self, out of safety, away from the known and the status quo—into what is in front of one: trial, danger, peril, risking what is out there.

(We can't know that s/he learns anything from experience; experience is just the happening itself, not the consequences.)

THE experience S/HE experiences and experiencING are all one, same:
(1) The path, way, life itself; (2) the leader, riskor, liver; and (3) the going first, stepping out, pressing forward are one
   = EXPERIRE: "The gift, the giver, and the giving are one."

The mind, intent, will, and psychic set of the actor AND the act of pressing forward toward the neumena (from the phenomenon) (see page xxx) ARE ONE with the consequence of the act: THE EXPERIENCE. Merely, with intent or will to "put your foot in the way."

THUS, EXPERIENCE = the wholly living person IS now on hir way, pilgrimage—HIR experience. Each step is filled with the unknown and risk. Life is to the living; s/he who steps forward resolutely on hir path is s/he who experiences. S/he who reads and studies is on the path of BEING student or scholar; s/he does NOT experience what s/he only reads ABOUT.

*

Changing now to a different tack, let us set "hypocrisy" as our target. We use that word to point at a church (commonly) to say "They don't practice what they preach." It's good that we all can see so clearly, but it's unfortunate that we don't catch what we have just said. Examine the usage carefully. Obviously, there appears to be a difference between what is done (actions, behavior) and what is said (propaganda, dogma, doctrines). For individual people, we indicate that what is believed is not the same as what is practiced. Psychology has brought that same truth home to us. There is, in fact, a vast difference between what one says and what s/he does. If we want to know what a person believes in, watch hir behavior, WATCH IT!—all of it, but don't listen to or be distracted by what s/he says (although that is also part of hir behavior). Transactional analysis says that people contaminate their communications with inflections, gestures, postures, and facial expressions. If we listen to the words as if they were spoken by an automaton, we miss the other and more true message. The real message of what a speaker is all about is to be found in the contamination.

So to conclude, don't listen to the propaganda, the party line, the ideology, the rationalizations, but WAKE UP and see (observe) the behavior, what s/he, in fact, does—hir response-ableness, where s/he puts hir time and psychic energy, and you will find the answer to what s/he is really all about. The same can be said for what the world is all about—or a group, a tribe, a society, a culture, a nation, a people— the TRUTH, once again.

The same applies to a church, club, or political faction. Don't fall for their doctrines and ideologies, but look at their behavior. Then you will know what they are all about, where they are going (if anywhere), and what their goals are.

Certainly you are now convinced that this is such a great tool for analysis of your environment. But it must also be applied to YOU. YOU have your own ideology, theories, doctrines, dogmas, rationalizations, and propaganda. You are the first person convinced by all this bull. We all have protections against the trash that others are forever laying on us. But we are engaged in kidding ourselves all the time. All our efforts to explain ourselves are made in order to convince SELF. It rarely takes in others although some may be OVERPOWERED. You are the one who buys your own party line. STUPID? WATCH IT! It is "by your fruits that ye are known."

You want to know what YOU stand for? Well, then shut up and WATCH IT! —your own behavior, all of it. You SAY that you're honest?

Forget that line of propaganda and tell me the last time you did not adhere precisely to the known. "How fast was that car going?" The only TRUTH is that you don't know, for YOU are not a speedometer. But you made a guess. When you repeat someone else's statement, do you KNOW what was in his or her mind at THE moment of speaking? But I'll bet you said that you KNEW what they said and repeated YOUR version. True honesty demands different behavior— or an admission of something less than honesty.

You have the God-given capacity to control your responses, the sum of all your behavior, IF you (WHO?) WILL simply take control of your organism. What stops you? The identity has the control, but it is NOT GOD; it IS limited. To try to respond in a WAY different from its basic conditioning is a terrible burden for the identity to carry. But WHAT stops YOU? It is your identity that has the problem. The definition of identity is the conditioned being: YOU. Thus to respond in the learned compulsive way is identical with the identity. So put down your burden (WHAT is that?) and take up your cross (what is THAT?). WHO?

CHAPTER VIII

God will answer all these questions for you. But God is NOT "out there." That is the process called externalization. It comes from the flat-earth god. But the truth now known is that God is "in here." Words that have been used for millennia to reference this concept include "Christ," "Buddha," and "center." You must turn to the center for all the answers to YOUR (WHO?) problems.

What IS your problem? There is only one problem TO have. It is the same problem that I have, that all people have and always have had (and always will have): the fact that the identity is limited. Your identity is clearly unique, one of a kind, never before existed, and never again to exist—and it is perfect good, OK. It was created by God, nature, fate, cosmic forces.

But by being unique, it is, by definition, not everything, all, infinite, or eternal. Its very uniqueness makes it limited, finite, mortal. So what does "God will solve the problem" mean, then? It translates, the Christ-center can control the responses of this organism. It is the center that has the response-ability.

Zen says it: Sit right down in the middle of your problem. WHO? Tie the word "middle" to the concept "center" and the word "problem" to the organism: Sit right down in the center of your organism. Thus, your consciousness sits at the center of your being. The requirement is, a command has been issued to the organism as follows:

(B) Sit down (and be physically submissive).

(C) Shut up.

(allow stillness—respect to King/God/Christ/Center).

(D) WATCH IT! Become aware of the makeup.

(and limitations) of your identity.

(E) Actualize the center's command over the organism.

Obviously, this is internalization. The identity has no control over the center, and it will resist this "taking command" operation. But that, in itself, is part of the makeup and limitations of the identity. WATCH IT!, remember, is THEWAY. The weapon or tool of the identity is rationalization. So hear the propaganda, but don't believe any of it. Listen deeply to why the line is being promulgated (by yourself). Every message is ideological rhetoric designed to maintain the status quo. Yes, this is true about societies, institutions, nations, and people. But it's also true about YOU. Remember, you don't fool anybody but yourself. So WATCH IT!

*

GNOSIS

```
            ( DO I HAVE TO  )
            ( [ MUST     ]  )
WHAT    ( [ OUGHT  ] I ) DO IN ORDER TO—
            ( [NEED       ]  )
                    ( [ACCOMPLISH  ]
            —TO  ( [ACHIEVE ]   MORE IN MY LIFE ?
                    ( [LIVE      ]    (    FULL    ) ?
                    ( MAKE MY LIFE)  MORE   (    COMPLETE )?
                                        (      ABUNDANT    )?
                                        (      SUCCESSFUL  )?
                                        (      SATISFYING  )?
                                        (      HAPPY         )?
                                        (      PLEASANT    )?
```

When one's behavior is to be put to the service of a goal,
then ONE MUST, of necessity, DO what those goals demand.
        (The actor is no longer free,
for s/he is in bondage to those demands.
        Those behaviors, which serve some other
goal, must be suppressed.)

HOWEVER, what one ACTUALLY DOES
will always be in CONFORMITY with what s/he CONCEIVES.
But what one conceives IS
UNDER THE CONTROL OF THE UNCONSCIOUS,
hir basic conditioning and not within hir consciousness.

$$
\begin{array}{ll}
& (\quad \text{OBTAIN} \quad) \\
\text{So you (WHO?) must} & (\quad \text{GENERATE} \quad) \text{ CONSCIOUS CONTROL—} \\
& (\quad \text{DEVELOP} \quad)
\end{array}
$$

—over the organism (which includes the identity),
both its physical and mental BEHAVIOR.
      (Mental behavior results in CONCEPTS.)

To do this requires, demands, the PRACTICE of AWARENESS:
awareness of Self and Self's responses, behavior.
One must awaken from sleep and step into the light.
      It is a long, hard WORK to OPEN your SELF:
There can be NO TRUTH,
NO CERTAINTY, in any CONCEPT, LAW, DOGMA, RULE.

IT IS A SOLO TRIP!

A guide may be of help,
but the responsibility lies SOLELY with the individual.
There is no single WAY/FOLLY/VANITY/TRIP
that is more valid than any other,
and they are all equally valuable.
All are limited to their narrow goal and are thus imperfect.
The ONLY WAY is AWARENESS and the PRACTICE
that brings CONSCIOUS CONTROL over ALL WAYS
and the emptiness of NOWAY.

When the IDENTITY becomes   (purposeless,)
                             (wayless,   )
                             (follyless,   )
                             (tripless,   )
                             (without [vanities,])
                             ([goals,   ])

it is then that the CENTER becomes ACTUALIZED
    (when the identity no longer controls the organism).
Then the spirit enters, the King reigneth, and the Beloved comes.

*

COMMENTARY ON HOW TO GET YOURSELF
TO DO WHAT YOU WANT TO DO
by PAUL E. WOOD

As children we are very lucky because parents make decisions for us and force us to change behaviors that are negative or self-destructive. So we become conditioned to look externally for the permission and the power to supervise our own behavior. When we become adults, there is no one outside ourselves who can apply this pressure to make change. Since we are response-able, we must give ourselves permission and use our own power.

Most people are prone to fuzzy thinking. In order to do something about one's condition, he MUST aim at concrete specificities: there is no way to find happiness or become happier. That is fuzzy, but one can have a specific target: to get up one hour earlier or lose ten pounds or stop smoking, etc.

Stop obsessing or agonizing over your vague feelings: change the behaviors. We must become aware of our habitual habits; they are controlled by the subconscious, and we must take conscious control. Changing some simple habit must become one's primary goal at that moment in life (so as to reinforce) success.

There is no such thing as "I can't [am incapable of] change." Demand proof of your inner sets, rationalizations, attitudes, and beliefs. Beliefs are our choice.

The procedure is
1. ELICIT all your ideas about why you do it or feel you can't do it;
2. EXAMINE each one in critical detail, requiring proof and hard data to support each idea;
3. ERODE each of the beliefs by an analytical examination; and
4. EXHAUST all the excuses so that there is nothing left to inhibit you or block you from changing.

Depression: the negative feeling that one is NOTOK, that the world is bad, that life is hopeless, that one is helpless. This one looks externally for help. But his problem is his inner attitude—and he can change that.

"I am going to try..." or "I am trying..." are statements of failure. "I have stopped..." is a statement of success. Wishes are in the same category: "I wish I were slimmer" = "I am not doing anything about it."

Analysis of why I do something (why do I act pig-parent toward my wife? Because I learned it from my father) is counterproductive and wrong-headed. Why? Because to make such analysis requires that the offensive behavior continues. One cannot continue to agonize over wrong behavior and stop the behavior at the same time. When one is no longer doing the thing, there no need to ask WHY one does it (since they aren't).

If you find yourself repeating a prohibited behavior, be careful to say, "I'm NOT stupid, dumb, weak, inept, or evil. I just wasn't paying attention [wasn't awake], and I made a mistake—PERIOD." Undo all the negative images with repetitive affirmations. Focus on your success, even success in being a bore or withdrawn or sloppy. See the good in the world and concentrate on that rather than its contrary. Give yourself credit for what you do right each time that you do it. Take credit for being successful.

Zero in on one really important aspect of your behavior that you want to change. It must be more important than anything else in your life and must be given your complete conscious attention. Stop worrying about all your other behaviors and feelings and focus on the big one you are now changing. Perhaps "the most important" can be found by studying what gives you the most pain, anxiety, fear, or trouble. It is not until every cell in your body is committed to a certain change that it will happen.

CONFRONT YOURSELF: (1) What is the exact, specific behavior I want to change? Is changing it right now more important than anything else in the world? (2) What evidence do I have that I am capable of making this change? Have I ever done it before? Have I ever successfully accomplished any behavior similar to what I want to do now? (3) What are the reasons and excuses that I have been using to avoid change and to maintain my position regarding this behavior? Do I have real evidence that my reasons are valid, or are they just assumptions, rationalizations, opinions, guesses. (4) Do I really need to change? What are the advantages of changing over staying just as I am? Am I willing to do whatever I have to change myself? (5) What have I been saying to myself which has prevented me from changing? Is this self-communication true or false?

We maintain the status quo—right within our own selves. If I, who hate the status quo, maintain it in myself, do I really want to change, or have I evolved a lifestyle that requires that status quo so I can go on being negative—complaining about its evil. So we keep (maintain) the same routines all the time and thus are the "living dead" (sound asleep).

How to handle stress? Contemplating a really important change creates stress within oneself. Relaxation and meditation are prime methods of handling stress. Fifteen to twenty minutes twice a day set aside in strategic time and place is not too much to give to your problem-self. Visualize the result you are aiming to attain.

Performance problems: the anxiety over performing and being judged. As we grow up we become sensitive to the judgments and reactions of others. We establish our view of ourselves from these others. If we are bombarded by negative criticism from the significant people in our lives, then we tend to see ourselves as inadequate. Some seek to overcome such feelings with hard work and success. Other people avoid any kind of competition or exposure; these frequently underachieve and often isolate themselves in safe niches where they feel secure. They avoid any kind of performance risk that will expose them as inadequate as they believe themselves to be. The result is low self-esteem (NOTOKness), loneliness, sadness, and depression.

Can you spare 2 percent of your available twenty-four hours? Are you worth investing half an hour in? To yourself?

*

Richard Wagner's *DIE WALKÜRE* :
    WOTAN (despairing, seeing himself as a failure as a God):
        "A free man creates himself. I can only create slaves."
        (for "slave" read: determined by conditioning)

(for "free" read: conscious control: response-able)
THUS: A man who freely exerts conscious control
over his organism creates himself.
"I [God, nature] can only create determined animals."
Wagner already knew in the late nineteenth century.

*

FREEDOM = FREE = FRE (Mid. Eng.) = FREO (Old Eng.)
from PRI (PIE): to love = PRIYO = FRIJAZ (Teut.) (AD 600)
   = FRI: love + -AZ
(AZ: -OS, -US, -UZ, -IS: s/he who or that which)
   = s/he who is loved = the beloved
(belonging to the loved ones)
THUS, s/he is NOT a slave = not in bondage = FREE
   = PRIY-ONT: loving = FRIJAND (Teut.): lover
   = FRIOND, FREOND (Old Eng.): FRIEND
(There you are, Friyands: Quakers)
   = PRI-TU = FRITHUZ (Teut.): peace = FRITH + UZ = AZ
FRITH (TH = D) = FRIDU (Old Ger.): peace
   = FRI + DHE: to lay down, put, set in place, make happen
THUS, s/he who establishes love
or the circumstances for love, which are peace
   = PRIYA (Sanskrit) (AD 200): dear, precious
   = PRI-YA: beloved = FRIJJO (Teut.): beloved, wife
   = FRIGG (Old Nor.): goddess of love
   = FRI: love + GHE: to release, make happen, go
THUS, s/he who releases love to those around hir
   (sharp *G* = Guh (FRIGG) or soft *G* = Juh (FRIJJ))
   = FRIGGE-DAEG (tag): FRIDAY
THUS, FREE = peace, love, precious, friend, AND thus NOT IN
BONDAGE + DOM = DHE: to set (dhe-n = down), put, place, THUS
establish, make happen.
THUS, FREEDOM is the establishment of peace (absence of conflict:
see humble, page xxx), love, preciousness, friendship, and thus one
not in bondage even to his conditioning.

CHAPTER IX

Now, let us relate all this to the religious tradition of Western civilization. Jesus said, "But thou, when thou prayest, enter into thy closet, and when thou hast shut the door, pray to the Father which is in secret"; and "Neither do men light a candle, and put it under a bushel [basket], but on a candlestick." Yes, your center is covered up by a basket; it sits there in your maintained darkness, like a bird in a covered cage: the identity covers the Christ-center and hides its light. Thus, you live your life in darkness—this is NOT belief; it logically follows from these basic concepts. The existence of the spark of life is hidden by BELIEF (love of pleasure: see page xxx) in the identity, which is the power that perpetuates it.

If we use Assagioli's (the Catholic psychiatrist and founder of psychosynthesis) metaphor and allow the inner energy to come out from under the cover to flow and act—BE—it will create newness, new behaviors, a whole new world of truth, joy, and light. Don't forget, the identity fears all this and will fight back. WATCH IT! and learn from its struggles. You are, and were, always OK. Don't let the identity's conviction that it is NOTOK dominate. Listen to its rationales, but don't swallow (believe) them—don't let IT fool you (WHO?).

Jesus indicated that the kingdom was not OF this world, that although he was IN the world, he was not OF it.

Translation: the Christ-center is IN this organism (location: we are IN the world), but not OF the organism (to the contrary, we are OF THEWAY, not a dependent follower of the identity and ITS way).

*

[Jesus speaks] "I go to prepare a place for you. And if I go and prepare a place for you, I will come again, and receive you unto myself; that where I am [present tense], THERE may ye be [present tense] also. And whither I go ye [already] know, and the way [WAY] ye know [since I have spent the last three years teaching you]."

[But disrespecting Jesus, contradicting his last statement] Thomas saith unto him, "Lord, we know not whither thou goest; and how can we know the way?"

Jesus saith unto him, "I am the way, the truth and the life: no man cometh unto the father, but by me. If ye had known me, ye should [have been smart enough to draw the conclusion that ye] have known my Father also: and from henceforth [from this immediate moment of my speaking] ye know [present tense = now] him, and have seen him [here and now: so the question is now answered for all time]."

[And now disagreeing and challenging,] Philip saith unto him, "Lord, shew us the Father, and it suffices us."

Jesus saith unto him, "Have I been so long time with you, and yet hast thou not known me? Philip! [And then he explains:] He that hath seen me hath seen the Father; and [accusingly] how [come] thou sayest then [since ye have seen me], Shew us the Father? Believest thou not [= do you deny] that I am in the Father and the Father in me? The words I speak unto you I speak not of myself: but the Father that DWELLETH in me, he doeth the works [speaketh the words, behave the behaviorisms]. Believe me that I AM in the Father, and the Father in me: or else believe me for the very works' sake. ["works' sake" = the truth you observe in the words and behaviorisms which I do.]" (JOHN 14:2–11)

DWELL: reside, fasten one's attention
    = DWELLEN (Mid. Eng.): to delay, linger, remain, reside
    = being influenced by DVELJA (same root)
       (Old Norse): sojourn, tarry
    = DWELLAN (Old Eng.): deceive, hinder, delay
    = DHEU (PIE): "to rise in a cloud" > vapor, smoke
       > breath and defective
    = perception clouded = DUSK: twilight or wits: DULL
    = DHUMO = FUMUS (Lat.); THUMOS (Grk.): soul, spirit
    = DHEUS = DUS (Teut.) = DYSIG: stupefied, confused
       > foolish > DIZZY
    = DOSE (Dan.): stupefy > make drowsy = DOZE
    = DHOUSA = DUKH (Slavic) = DUKH (Russ.): breath, spirit
    = DHWES = DHWENS = DUNS (Teut.) = DUST; bird's DOWN
    = DHUS = THUOS (Grk.): burnt sacrifice, incense
    = DHEUBH: senses beclouded = DHOUBHO = DAUBAZ (Teut.):
       DEAF
    = DHUMBHO = DUMBAZ (Teut.): DUMB
    = DHWEL = DWELAN (Teut.): to go or lead astray
    = DWELLAN (Old Eng.): to deceive

THUS, DHEU = DHWEL = DWELL: a cloud of vapor, smoke, fume, breath > soul, spirit > burnt sacrifice, incense, dusk, dust, that impedes perception SO THAT one becomes beclouded in the senses > stupefied, confused, foolish > dizzy, deaf, dumb. The CAUSE IS external; the perceiver is influenced, led to fasten hir attention, THUS led astray, deceived, hindered, delayed (beguiled), AND THUS lingers, remains, tarries, sojourns > resides because s/he is so beguiled.

DWELL carries the meaning that something resides because its attention is captured so that its leaving is delayed, hindered, diverted, beguiled, and thus it lingers, remains, tarries there until that external influence wanes or is eliminated. That which fastens the attention is the essence of DWELL for without it the subject would not be resident there at all.

"The Father DWELLETH in me" = the Father lingers, tarries in me as long as his/its attention is riveted on its own purpose for being there—whatever that influence may be—and will not reside there one moment longer.

THUS, the Father is beclouded in HIR senses, stupefied, confused by the smoke, DUST of the soul s/he lingers in. And I remain just as long as S/HE chooses to be interested—rivet hir attention—in being within this beclouding distraction: ME.

"For dust thou art, and unto dust shalt thou return" = thou art that smoke, vapor, breath, spirit that beclouds man's perception.

SO what is MAN? = HUMAN = HUMANUS (Lat.)
    = DHGHEM (PIE): earth (both soil and the planet)
    = DHGHOMO = HUMUS: ground, soil = HUMBLE, HUMILITY: low, base
    = DHGHOMON: earthling = HOMO (Lat.): human being, man = HOMBRE
S/HE is made out of earth and one of the residents of earth.

Basic root DHE (PIE): to set, put > lay down
    > establish, make happen, firm = DO, DEED, DOOM, -DOM, DEEM;
    = (Lat.) FACERE: to make; FACIES : shape, FACE
    = DHGHM = DHE + GHE + M
    = DHE: to set, put, lay down, establish, deem, judge, create
    = GHE: to let go, release, put into action
    = ME: (*a*) to measure > think, mind, memory (the soul at work)
        (*b*) in the middle of me > an individual soul,
           spirit (measuring, thinking)
DHGHM: establish the release of the individual soul thinking;
      the place where the release of the individual soul
        thinking is established;
     to put into action the establishment
        of the individual soul thinking;
     the place where the establishment of the individual soul
        thinking is put into action;

ADAM = HA-DAM-A (Heb.): earth—(DAM > DHGHM)

THUS, our authority, Jesus, tells us that the eternal, omnipresent God of the tradition dwells, resides in this organism, HUMAN, defined as that individual thinking soul who has been released into action.

*

It is said that Christ came into the world to save it. Translate: the Christ-center(point) came into this organism to save IT (WHO?). No, this concept of a savior does not arise in order to save the identity; it comes to save the WORLD (WER-ALDH, see page xxx): the whole organism and its history, not the arrogant identity.

It is said by Paul (in Corinthians), "Know ye not that ye are the Temple of God and that the Spirit of God dwelleth in you?" and "What? Know ye not that your body is the Temple of the Holy Ghost which is in you, which ye have of God?" and "For ye are the Temple of the living God; as God hath said, I will dwell [*] in thee and walk in them." Paul is not saying something mystical requiring some stretch or strain of belief. He is simply saying the TRUTH that all religions have promoted.

Matthew used a metaphor most powerful when he described "Jesus, when he had cried again in a loud voice, yielded up the ghost. And behold, the veil of the temple was rent in twain from the top to the bottom." That curtain, which had hidden the holy of holies from the profane eyes of man (homo) was not just lifted or opened; it was DESTROYED, and the inner secrets exposed by the act of this man Jesus, FOREVER. The death of Jesus (the eradication of his organism) IS the destruction of the veil, which hides that inner secret and discloses the Christ for all to see.

Paul (again in Corinthians) applies this to "every man" when he argues, "But even unto this day, when Moses [the Torah, the Old Testament] is read, the veil is upon their [the children of Israel] heart [center]. Nevertheless when it [that heart] shall turn to the Lord [WHO?], the veil shall be taken away."

*

Incidentally, the name Jesus is incorrect. It is properly Yeshuah. Since he made it a point to insist that his name was important, one should be careful to get it right. Why? He said that the first commandment was to love God, who to the Jews (and Jesus) at that time was YHWH, a name not to be pronounced. In order to pronounce such words, one must supply vowels. To do so is arrogant. "Humble" refuses to unconsciously supply vowels, and then the word IS unpronounceable.

Yeshuah is spelled in the ancient Hebrew (and Aramaic) as YHSWH, the same YHWH with an additional S placed in the CENTER: YH S WH. That S (pronounced "sh") is the symbol for earth—the world—"hereness" and "nowness," and changes YHWH (I AM THAT I AM) to YHSWH (I AM ON EARTH THAT I AM). Thus the name Yeshuah is correctly translated: "I am that which I am, here and now, on earth—in this world." YSHWH IS "in here" NOW and forever.

YAM, HERE on this planet, NOW, in existence as YAM.

YHSWH = YAM the "suchness" of all on earth.

It is that divine energy flowing out from the human and acting on the world, hir environment (and hir neighbors)—which is the leaven, the yeast, which makes the bread rise (gives life to the organism). The lump of tasteless dough is changed (in the twinkling of an eye) by that energy flow into something of value—NEW, nourishing, and tasty bread.

Likewise, "Ye are the salt of the earth, but if the salt has lost its savor, wherewith shall it [the earth] be salted?" The environment is likened unto a soup, and s/he WHO? sits within hir organism is likened unto the salt that makes the soup tasty and desirable. These are the saviors of the world and the conduit though which God acts to make whatever S/HE wills—WILL, as per Assagioli.

*

Here is a WAY to show the depth difference between true religion and organized religion, between the truth and dogma, substance, spirit, and the letter of the law. Jesus says in, Matthew 16:6, 12,

"Beware of the leaven [doctrines] of the Pharisees... Sadducees," "Ye are the leaven," "By your fruits are ye known," The Kingdom of Heaven is at hand," etc. We (modern Western man) read that we ARE to be and that we SHOULD be (but that way is guilt). The Christian is supposed to be the leaven. This way misreads the truth that Jesus brought. He said, "Ye ARE...!"

All people are stimuli in this world. Every act (and non-act), behaviorism, is an input into the consciousnesses of everyone else. We, each and every and at all times, are a leaven. Our inputs enliven the community, make it boil, stew, and grow. We have no choice. What Jesus was saying was that we OUGHT (it is smart if we) become aware and accept the TRUTH that we ALREADY ARE the leaven. There is no alternative. There is only (*a*) choice of awareness (or blind sleep) and (*b*) choice of behaviors (response-ability, see page xxx). We can only choose, through will, the stimuli we input into the world.

Jesus pointed to the truth. Western Christian guilt says that he (divine) brought truth we cannot know. Wrong! Jesus (the man) brought the truth that has always been true, but we turn away from it. We don't want to hear the truth that burns and condemns us. Therefore, we deprecate Jesus, turn AWAY from him, and turn TO the divine illusion. We DENY that which we already KNOW (just like Peter).

If we respect the god that sent us that fantastic man of knowledge who helps us to see ourselves, the world, and God clearly, then we must respect him—Jesus, the true man—not some pie-in-the-sky god. Jesus brought us reality: that in which we live, move, and have our being. That kingdom IS—we need not BELIEVE it nor need we adhere, love, or worship it; we need only recognize that it IS, always WAS, and ever WILL BE, whether we are ignorant and asleep or not. It doesn't depend on what we BELIEVE; it doesn't matter even WHETHER we believe—it merely IS.

The truth (which sets us free) brought by Jesus is as concrete as that the earth is spherical, that the sun rises each day, that the moon circles the earth, and that we need and get oxygen from the air around us.

*

What does it mean to "die to self and be reborn"? If this organism, once commanded by the identity, is now commanded by the Christ-center, then the identity has been set aside on the shelf and no longer can be seen by others. The basket has been removed, and the light shines now for, and on, all. The old self is no longer—it EXISTS NO LONGER. But the organism still lives, like unto a rebirth with a new center of organization, with a new agenda to live by, and a new WAY: a new personality, a new persona: a new person.

There are those people who hew tightly to the "straight and narrow" path, WAY, as contrasted with those who thrash and squirm, trying Zen, monasticism (commune), then politics (both the right and the left are, by definition, off the path), and finally hedonism or some other sort of broad, easy way.

What has HUMILITY to do with all this? The answer lies in first finding its antonym: arrogance.

ARROGANT: overbearingly proud, haughty, self-important
from ARROGANS (Lat.) pp. of ARROGARE: to claim for oneself
= AD: to + ROGARE: to ask
from REG: to move or direct in a straight line
      THUS, to move or direct something straight > correctly
THUS, to lead or rule competently
    = REG-TO (Teut.) = REHTAZ (-AZ: s/he who or that which)
    = RIHT (Old Eng.) = RIGHT
    = REGERE (Lat.): lead straight, guide, rule = RECTUS: right
    = RIGYO (Celt) = RIKYA (Teut.): king = REICH (Ger.): kingdom
    = REX (Lat.): king, REGAL, ROYAL
    = REG-EN = RAJAN, RAJA (Sanskrit): RAJAH: he rules
    = ROG = RAKO (Teut.): RAKE:
      a thing with straight pieces of wood
    = RANKAZ (Teut.) = RANC (Old Eng):
      strong, haughty, overbearing, RANK
    = RANKINAZ (Teut.): ready, straightforward
    = GE-RECENIAN: to arrange in order = RECKON
    = ROGA, ROGARE (Lat.):
      to stretch out the hand straightly > to ask
THUS, ROGARE = to stretch out one's hand for that which one straight out, overbearingly, haughtily, regally asks as a matter of right

as if s/he were the ruler, the king; THUS s/he DEMANDS something OUTRIGHT.

AD-ROGATE: AD: to + REG = s/he demands it to hirself

ABROGATE: AB: away + REG = to abolish by fiat

DEROGATE: DE: down and away + REG =
    to detract, restrict, belittle

PREROGATIVE: PRAE: before + REG =
    to ask successfully before the others

SUBROGATE: SUB: instead of + REG =
    to nominate an alternative candidate

THUS, ARROGATE is to demand or claim something for one's self outright as belonging to hir BY RIGHT.

HUMILITY: being humble, lacking pride,
    modesty, submission, self abasement;
    this is a stance that one takes for oneself

HUMILIATION: to lower another's pride, dignity, status:
    to humble, degrade, disgrace
    thus, to make another inferior or feel inferior.

Both from HUMBLE: modest, meek, lowly, unpretentious, abase or abased; the opposite of pride.

SYNONYMS: lack of pride, pretense, or assertiveness

from (h)UMBLE (Old Fr.) from HUMILITIS (Lat.): low, lowly, base

from HUMUS: ground, soil from DHGHEM: earth (see page xxx)

DHGHEM = (dh) GHM-ON = GUMON (Teut.) = GUMA (Old Eng.) = GROOM: man

    = DHGHOM = KHTHON (Grk.): earth (both soil and planet)

    = DHGHM = KHAMAI (Grk.): on the ground, down, low, lowly

    = DHGHOM-O = (dh) (g) HOMO = HUMUS (Lat.): earth, soil

    = HOMO (Lat.): one of the earth (dust?), earthling

THUS, HUMBLE = earth dweller, native, HUMAN being, mankind.

THUS, HUMBLE is not necessarily of the lowest (as distinguished from the highest) but rather one of nature's basic, fundamental earthy men, salt of the earth, not of some illusory aristocracy of the world—meaning, without pretense, illusion or delusions of grandeur or greatness; not special, not distinguishable from the mass of people; without privilege of rank, status, money, position; without some special dispensation even from God, such as talent, family or associations. Humble is not inferior but absolutely without possible claim to superiority, or even equality with anything. This is the natural condition of all humanity.

If one is not humble, it follows then that s/he is arrogant. If we relinquish the identity's arrogance to the center, we (WHO?) are then humble. The "we" is the identity, which is unable to create anything. It is God who is the creator, by definition. Hir energy, command is no longer repressed and altered after the identity (devil?) is unseated from the throne of command over the organism.

Why do we find some kind of superiority so necessary in our lives? It is obviously to cover an imperative feeling of inferiority, which we wrongly conclude in infancy. Then our dependence and lack of ability to cope with our environment led us to believe that we were inferior. And our environment did not belie that conclusion.

The subject of arrogance has been dealt with clearly: "Blessed are the meek, for they shall inherit the earth."

MEEK: patient, humble,
    long-suffering (nonhostile), kind, gentle
    from ME-K = MEOC (Mid. Eng.) from MJUKR (Old Nor.)
    (Meeuhcker): soft
    from MEUG: to act surreptitiously, skulk, mooch
    from MEU: damp, shiny, slippery
    also MEUNG = MUNGERE (Lat.): to blow one's nose
  = Sh-MUG: SMOCK, SCHMUCK: adornment = SMUG
  = MUGGA: drizzle = MUGGY
  = Sch-MOCKeln = SMOKELEN: smuggle
  = MYGLA = MOLD, MILDEW
    also MEUK = MYKI, MYKR = MUCK
  = MJUKR: soft = MEEK
  = MEUKUS (Lat.) = MUCUS: moist, musty
    also MUK = MUKUS: fungus, MUSHroom

THUS, from the roots gathered:
    damp, shiny, slippery, drizzle, wet,
    mildew, muck, moist, musty, mucus

MEUG is wet, rotting, slippery, and smelly
MUK: fungus—mushrooms grow in damp, moist, mucky ground
    act surreptitiously, skulk, mooch, smuggle
    a smuggler moves slippery at night in the swamps
    fancy adornment, jewels, smug, schmuck
    a smug schmuck: a smelling rotten piece of dirt (shit)
    and MEEUCK: soft = MEEK is soft and yielding

THUS, MEEK is soft, yielding, and forgiving—a hit or stroke (of sword) at the MEEK sinks in mushy without leaving a mark; s/he doesn't respond with HARD, resistant, hostile, fighting behavior, nor does s/he fear and flee (neither fight nor flight): s/he is yielding and accepts all strokes—MUCUS, MUNG, MUSH, and MUCK are not injured by the stroke (cut water and after you remove your blade there is no visible mark). After a verbal hostile attack on MEEK, there will not be any visible response that s/he was injured in any way.

Does MEEK have slippery, surreptitious ends or purposes in mind and intent? S/he might well be suspicioned of smuggling; s/he is carrying the light, the truth, love. But s/he (WHO?) does not show even this by behavior. It is the spirit that acts through the MEEK. The absence of visible behavior by MEEK allows the spirit to shine forth.

The meek are the willing (for whatever motivations) to relinquish their claim to any part of their world. And when the identity so humbly steps aside, arrogance is dead and the spirit flows out into the world through the Christ-center.

CHAPTER X

Following Assagioli's concept, God speaks through the Christ-center to man (homo) directly that energy flow issues from within (location) the individual and affects the organism as it does so, NOW. If, on the contrary, God speaks through a book, will WHO? translate, interpret, or define the words? WATCH IT!

The identity is limited in its understanding (remember, by definition, it IS limited). We are advised to listen to an intuitive voice. WATCH IT! Is that voice the center speaking or an archetype? WHO? speaks? Can the identity ever be certain who the speaker is? NO! The wrong center of organization is still trying to maintain its hold over the organism: stay in command. But the Christ-center cannot be wrong (by definition, again).

So now you know the meaning of "surrender to God": give command of the organism to the Christ-center. WATCH IT! "Give" betrays the fact that the identity is doing an act called giving and thus still remains the God: el benefactor. "Surrender" means to "yield" over the control and command of something to the other. It is precisely the military term in which the commander yields his organ, tool, army to another. The identity hands over command of the organism of the Christ-center.

Shall we then be gods ourselves? Ask yourself, can YOU (WHO?) make your-self into a God? You KNOW that THAT is impossible. You do not have the power. For the identity to act as if it were God is for it to be the Antichrist. WATCH IT! You can so easily be bogged down in the linguistic traps here. "Ye shall be as Gods." WHO? Who is making who into a God? (WHO? created us [WHO?] as Gods!) If we try to make the identity a better, purer commander of the organism, we are creating the identity as God (with clay DHGHM feet). But we have already done that. The identity has been in command of the organism for all your life already, and you have gone nowhere at all. The identity has been the god for the organism all the while. Why don't we think of stopping that system and starting ANEW?

This is where we all start on the path, WAY. The basic issue is to STOP the identity from playing God and allow Christ to act in and through us. Translate that religious jargon: to have the Christ-center come into command of the organism.

SCIENCE OF MIND: 1990, May 7: HAPPINESS by Norma A. Hawkins:

"If there were two creators their wills would clash and there would be no order, no system, no harmony—", only conflict, clash, noise, anger, hate and resentment at the conflicts very existence.

In fact, there ARE two creators: (1) the Cosmic Energy (WHO?) that created both this organism and its context, milieu in which it "lives, moves and has its being" ; AND (2) this identity now superimposed on this organism and this identity's world. And between these two there IS dissonance (cognitive). It is we ourselves who created this conflict; and we can't stand our own failure to end it. Thus we eternally pray for peace to end the conflict. We pray to something outside ourselves for the cure while we spend most of our psychic energy maintaining the identity and thus the conflict.

"—happiness is not something we can find outside ourselves; rather it is the awareness of our unity with Something greater than ourselves."

So whose intuitive voice IS speaking? We are afraid to surrender to it. "We" is the little frightened identity, the infantile child of our maturing life. So let us set aside our childish (read infantile) ways (as distinguished from THEWAY) and become a HUMAN (not homo). "Fear not" has been said for millennia (read the book and SEE) in order to still the identity's fears and reassure the child. WHO? shall still those fears?

If God is to command this organism, then the identity must stand out of the WAY. The usual metaphor is to ask God for guidance and await the Word. Thus, the identity demands that the WORD be processed through hir-self so that s/he might supervise the message. But when the identity is out of the WAY and the word acts directly; there is no identity in existence to translate the message. The medium (the organism as it is controlled: "By thy fruits, ye shall be known") IS the message (and the massage). If I truly believe in the will of God, then it follows that I (the identity) CANNOT KNOW that WILL, for THAT will is apprehended only through the ACT of the Christ-center. WHO? DOES command this organism, anyway.

*

CARNAL: desire and appetites of the flesh or body
THUS, sensual, animal
THUS, worldly, earthly, nonspiritual, not holy or sanctified
    = CARNALIS = CARD with stem CARN-: flesh = SKER (PIE)
        also SEK (SKE-): to cut (Lat.) + SECARE: to cut = SICKLE
SKER = SEK + KER = SKER: to cut
SHEAR, SHARE, SCAR, SCORE, SHEARS, SHARD, SHORT,
SHIRT, SKIRT, SKIRmish, SCREEN
        (s)KAR = CARO = CARnage, CARnival, CARRion, CROne,
CARnivorous, inCARnate
KORYO = CORIUM: leather (piece of flesh)
KR-TO = CURTUS: short = CURT
KORT = CORTEX: that which can be cut off like bark
    = SCAB, SCURF, SHARP, SCARF, SCARP, SCRAPE,
      SCRUB, SHRUB, SCROBIS: Trench, SCREW
    also SKER: to leap or jump for joy, turn and bend, wither,
SHRINK, crease and fold, wrinkle, spine, back,
KURWO = CURVUS: CURVE

also SKER: excrement, dung: cut off and separated from the body
also SKERI: to cut, separate, sift, wrinkle
    = SCRATCH, incise, SCRIBE, write, writing,
    = (s)CRIMEN: to write down a judgment
    = (s)KERIEIN: to sift, separate, decide, judge = CRITIC
      also SKERU: to cut, a cutting tool: SCREW

THUS, the root CARO is a bloody cut-off piece of flesh, cut off from God and separated freshly from the body (of God); it still twitches, jumps about, as if it had life and will—but only as a reflex action = subconscious control. It is truly unconscious.

INCARNATION = INCARNATE: to give bodily form to
    = INCARNARE (Lat.): to make flesh
    = IN: causitive + CARO (stem CARN): flesh
    = to make in or bring into the flesh (CARO)
It now becomes clear that something is brought to DWELL in that bloody quivering piece of meat that jumps about as if it had life.

For that flesh to be reborn, there must be a resurrection. "RESURRECTION" is the word chosen by the King James scholars to translate from the Greek ANASTASIS = ANA + STASIS. And it is an incorrect translation.

RESURRECTION = RESURRECT: to bring back to life—passive
    = RESURRECTUS pp. of RESURGERE (Lat.):
      to resurge: to rise again (active)
    = RE: again + SURGERE (Lat.): SURGE: to lead straight up
      > to rise and heave up violently
    = SUB: up from under + REGERE: to lead, rule, command
    = REG: to move in a straight line > straight
    >corRECT, RIGHT, REX, RAJAH, REICH
THUS, this is an active force that moves straight up from under (in the grave). Thus, it is incorrect to say that Jesus was resurrected (passive), rather he actively RESURGED, violently heaved straight up, undeviatingly, from under.

ANASTASIS = ANA + STASIS
ANA (Grk.):   up, upward, upward progression
again: up, upward, upward progression
again, renewal; in accordance with
        (intensification)
back, backward, reversed, reversion (perhaps incorrect)
    = AN (PIE): on, ON; other (of two); confused with AN = aNE: not
      (the other, thus not this)

ANABAPTIST: one who is rebaptized (as an adult)
  = ANA: again + BAPTEIN (Grk.): to dip
  = GWEBH (PIE): to dip, sink (in Grk.: GWE > B + BH > P = BAP)
THUS, ANA-: the Anabaptists' opponents simply saw this as a re-(again) baptism. But to be baptized is also renewal, rebirth according to Christ's intent; it intensifies life, and it is a reversion to our condition in Paradise or at birth before being tarnished by our family of origin.

ANABASIS: military advance = ANABAINEIN (Grk.):
a going up or forward = ANA: up + BAINEIN: to go
  = GWA (PIE): to go, come
  = BEMA (Grk.): step, seat, raised platform
  = GWMYO = BAINEIN: go, walk, step
  = GWMTI = BASIS: a stepping, tread, base
THUS ANA-: a going forward is also a going onward
    Thus, up on > upon

ANACHRONISM: something out of place or time, incongruity
  = ANAKHRONIZEIN (Grk.) = ANA: backward, reversed
  + KHRONIZEIN: belonging to a particular time = KHRONOS:
    time, THUS ANA-: the negative aNE: not timely

ANALECTS: selections of parts of literary works
  = ANALEKTOS: choice, selection = ANALEGEIN (Grk.)
  = ANA: up + LEGEIN = LEG (PIE): to collect, gather
THUS ANALECTS: to select up out of the collection.
THUS ANA-: up > out ALSO the negative: not in the collection

ANALOGY: correspondence between two otherwise dissimilar items
  = ANALOGOS (Grk.): proportionate, resembling
  = ANA: according to (the other)
  + LOGOS (Grk.): proportion, word = LEGEIN (Grk.): speak
  = LEG (PIE): gather
THUS, ANA-: OTHER of two = resembling the other, in accord, matched.

ANALYSIS: separation of the whole
into its constituent parts or elements
  = ANALUSIS (Grk.): a releasing = ANALUEIN: to undo (untie)
  = ANA: back + LUEIN: to loosen = LEU (PIE): divide, cut apart
THUS, ANALYSIS: to cut apart into its constituent elements
THUS, ANA-: (the intensive) to divide absolutely.

ANATHEMA: an ecclesiastical curse; excommunication
  = (Lat.): a curse, offering = (Grk.): votive offering
  = ANATITHENAI: to dedicate = ANA: up + TITHENAI: to put
THUS, ANATHEMA: to put up (on the alter) = to offer up
THUS, ANA-: up on ALSO a curse is the reverse of a dedication

ANATOMY = the science of organic structure = ANATOME (Grk.)
  = ANATEMNEIN: to dissect
  = ANA: up + TEMNEIN: to cut = TEM (PIE): cut
THUS, ANA-: (cut) up, meaning apart—into pieces

THUS, ANA-: again > renewal, rebirth;
ANA-: up, up on, upon; up out; forward, onward;
ANA-: sets apart; (select) out: (negative) not in
ANA-: in accordance with the other of two,
  resembling the other
ANA-: (cut) up, apart absolutely (intensification);
ANA-: opposite, reversal

THUS, ANA-: UP, ON, upon, onward; upward, upward progression;
  (set) apart, (select) out: (negative): not in;
  again, renewal, rebirth;
  in accordance with the other;
  (cut) up, apart absolutely (intensification);
  opposite, reversal (the other, not this)

STASIS: stagnation, motionlessness
  = (Lat.): slowing, or stopping, a stable state
   or balance, equilibrium
  = (Grk.): a standing, a standstill = STA (PIE): to stand
  = ST@ = STETI = STASIS

= STETO = STATOS (Grk.): placed, standing (still) = STATIC
(-OS = -AZ: s/he who or that which—is standing.)
= STETA = STAT-ES (Grk.): s/he who causes a standing
= STAU-RO = STAUROS (Grk.): cross, post (it is standing)
= ST = SIST = HISTANAI, STANAI (Grk.): to set, place
= APOSTASY, ECSTACY
= HISTOS: that which is set up > web, tissue
= STOWA = STOA (Grk.): porch: the pillared area without seats
outside the house. The place where everybody stood to talk
outside the temples. Zeno the Stoic taught on the porch.
= STOIC: unmoving, free of passion
= STO = STULO = STULOS (Grk.): pillar = STYLITE

THUS, STASIS is motionless and stagnant but is not dead, laying down; it is a thing in its place, standing in equilibrium, balanced, stable, thus motionless—but waiting, centered (not sleeping).

THUS, ANA-STASIS is
a STASIS that has ended and now moves up, upward,
          in an upward progression;
absolutely separate, distinct, opposite STATUS cut out from,
a reversal of, and clearly other than the previous STASIS
now no longer in equilibrium, balanced, stable, motionless;
a renewal, rebirth (again) of what was
before the STASIS and in accordance with it.

THUS, ANASTASIS = that upward thrusting force that terminates STASIS, stability, equilibrium and balance and is its absolute opposite: a renewal and rebirth of ACTIVITY that ends the motionlessness and stagnation; RESURRECTION is that active force that moves violently straight up undeviatingly, from under.

THUS, we are talking about that force boiling up within the human that agitates hir to SURGE UP OUT of hir own STASIS into the unknown that brings hir so much anxiety and pain (see EXPERIENCE, page xxx). And is also the intense, clearly OTHER, dynamic individual thrusting UP from under (oppression) that is the antithesis of the status quo (the existing state of society) and is the leaven that makes the culture dynamic.

*

"Rise, take up thy bed and walk!"

JESUS to scribes says, "[Is it] easier to say 'Thy sins be forgiven thee'; or to say: 'Arise and walk?" (Matthew 9:5); "Arise, and take up thy bed, and walk? " (Mark 9:2); "But that ye may know that *the Son of Man* hath power on earth to forgive sins (then saith he) Arise, take up thy bed and go unto thine house" (Matthew 9:6); "I say unto you, Arise, and take up thy bed and go thy way into thine house" (Mark 2:11); "Rise, take up thy bed and walk [it being the Sabbath, it was not lawful to carry a bed]" (John 5:11).

ARISE: to get up, move upward, ascend; originate,
come into being (birth) = ARISAN (Old Eng.) = RISAN
RISE: get out of bed; move from a lower to a higher position; extend upward; to be erected, to become stiff, erected; uplift oneself (to meet the challenge), to return to life
    = RISE, ROSE, RISEN = RISEN, ROS, RISEN (Mid. Eng.)
    = RISAN, RAS, RISEN (Old Eng.) = RISAN (Teut.): RISE, REAR, RAISE
    = RISAN from ER (PIE): to set in motion
    = AR (Teut.): to be, exist > ARE, ART
    = ARNJAOST (Teut.): EARNEST, serious, ardor
    = ERNEST: vigor in battle
    = ORIRI (Lat.): to arise, appear, be born > ORIGIN
    = REI: to flow, RUN > RILL = RIVUS (Lat.): stream > RIVER
    = REINO = RENOS (Gaul): river > RHINE
    = ERGH: go = ORGHEYO = ORKHEISTHAI (Grk.): dance > ORCHESTRA
    = ER + GHE: to release, let go = to release into motion
THUS, ARISE, RISE = to put one's Self into action and thus into existence, to begin to flow, dance, to make vigorous appearance in the scene, seriously impacting on the environment, THUS to lift oneself up to meet the challenges of life, THUS coming into being, returning to life—having been reborn, THUS awakening to true consciousness.

TAKE UP: to raise, lift

BED: a place where one sleeps
    = BHEDH (PIE): to dig > garden plot, sleeping place
    = BHE: to warm > BATH, BAKE
    + DHE: set, put > lay down, establish
    = BHEDH: an established warm place of nurture or security.
THUS, BED is the place you have established as warm and secure where you may continue habitually asleep: unawake, unaware, unconsciously controlled.

WALK: to go on foot; roam about, stroll
    to conduct oneself or behave in a particular manner:
social class or occupation: walk of life
    = WALKIEN (Mid. Eng.) = WEALCAN (Old Eng.): to roll, toss, roll up
    = WEL 3 (PIE): turn, roll
    = WALTZ; WALLON (Ger.): roam; VOLVERE (Lat.): roll; VALLEY
THUS, WALK is not merely to put one foot in front of another but rather to conduct one's manner of life or behavior by moving through one's world, environment, or surroundings in such a way: consciously and responsibly chosen walk of life: social class, profession, occupation. Not some way proposed by a religion (external authority), but Jesus proposed, the Father, and the kingdom being within that one do that which s/he wants to receive (reap), a self-chosen way.

THUS: "Rise, Take up thy bed and walk!"

RISE! = Put one's Self into action and meet life's challenges: flow, dance, and make vigorous and serious impact on the environment, THUS truly come into being, be reborn and awaken to true consciousness.
TAKE UP THY BED—: Take control over that established, secure place where you have been asleep, unawake, unaware, and unconsciously controlled;
—AND WALK!: Move through your environment in some social role in a consciously and responsibly self-chosen behavior or way, in which you do that which you want to receive.

THUS, Jesus commanded to PUT one's Self into action and meet life's challenges—flow, dance, and make vigorous and serious impact on the environment, THUS truly come into being, be reborn, and awaken to true consciousness! TAKE control over that established, secure place where you have been asleep, unawake, unaware, and unconsciously controlled; AND MOVE through your environment in some social role in a consciously and responsibly self-chosen behavior or way, in which you do that which you want to receive.

ASCEND = ASCENDERE (Lat.) = AD: to, toward + SCANDERE: to climb
   = SKAND: to leap = SCALAE: steps, ladder
   = to climb toward or to (active, assertive, aggressive)

LEVITATE, LEVITY, LEVER, LIGHTEN: lack of weight, lightness
   = LEVITAS: raises easily
   = LEVARE (Lat.): raise = LEVIS (leghwis) = LEGWHI
   = LEGWH: having little weight = LE-GWH
   = LEI (PIE): to let go, slacken, allow + GWER: heavy
THUS, take off the weight, lift the guilt with permission,
   and IT (WHO?) rises automatically.

To "rise up to God in heaven," to "ascend the Shushumna," and to "raise oneself to higher powers, matters, planes," etc., are equivalents. But we do not passively await forces beyond ourselves to act, but instead, we actively and aggressively tackle or wrestle with the problem ourselves (Jacob's ladder and his wrestling went together)—one process.

CHAPTER XI

And so we come to the subject of authority. To get some perspective, we note that there are some rules of nature that MUST come before—are in fact superior to—God. Such things as 2 + 2 = 4; that circular reasoning proves nothing (the Bible is true because it says so in the Bible); symbology (words stand for concepts); semantics; linguistics; psychology—above all the study and knowledge (logos) of how the human mind works.

If we insist that the Bible is the Word of God, by that process of insisting, we have made ourselves the authority, the God. The truth of our statement lies in ourSELF; it is true because WE say it is. This is primary in testing any of our beliefs. We (WHO?) are the authority of truth: we author it. Even when we look to a special message from God himself as our authority, still the only WAY to prove (even to ourselves) that it was God who spoke is through the belief (what we want to be true) that what was perceived was God speaking (and not an hallucination). That it WAS God is still based on our own authority, is still circular reasoning, and thus proves nothing—NOTHING at all. (Thus, we repress doubt, and project it, to satisfy our egos.)

And if I am the authority, then I have denied God—denied to God the ability to speak to man directly, other than through the Bible. WHO? am I to dictate that God CANNOT DO something? In order for me to deny God an ability is to make myself the authority figure and thus the God. Our whole intellectual way, in this scientific age, has been to arrogantly arrogate to ourselves the authority to be the author of the Antichrist: s/he who has arrogated to hirself the authority, the author of the truths to be found in the world.

The first sin is the shift of responsibility to the "out there" authority, such as the Bible. We actually make our own choice of belief, but then refuse to take the response-ability for that choice. We put the blame "out there" because we are terribly afraid that we just might be wrong and thus very guilty about a very important matter. So we blame the book or blame the church in the same way that Eve blamed the snake and the twentieth-century Germans blamed the Nazis. When we really do wish to believe a specific passage out of the Bible, let us take the response-ability and not shift the blame "out there," but KNOW (be aware) that we make our own choices, be willing to live with them and accept their consequences (what we reap).

God is the author of the LOGOS—WORD—and thus the truths of (note: not IN) the Bible. If that be true, then our poor, weak, limited identity is UNABLE to know the truth. Homo is so filled with ambivalences that s/he cannot know what truth is. S/he demands even inconsistencies to be true because S/HE WANTS IT that way so very badly; they frighten hir so. Our way is the way of the schizoid intellect, which originated in the Reformation and its coordinate scientific age. To determine truth, we must look to the Christ-center. It was said that Jesus spoke with a new authority. So if s/he is to be the model, then when dealing with these matters or attempting to interpret one of the scriptures, let each of us speak with a new authority ourSelves—WATCH IT! WHO? is determining the truths to be found there.

"Jesus" is a symbol—simply a word—which is a label attached by his parents and sociocultural group to a homo who ran around the Middle East about AD 30. "Christ" is another symbol—for an incarnation, a living God—which is eternal and not tied to any culture or time. Thus "Jesus Christ" is not a first and last name, but rather the conjunction of two separate concepts. Thus, was it that identity (Jesus) that spoke with the new authority? Or was it the divine center actualized in the man, which authored the new? This question demands that we examine exactly what we DO worship in the Christian religion.

"Worship" was taken from European feudalism by the King James scholars circa 1585. It is a label for the act of fealty performed by a vassal to hir "lord" in realizing their contractual relationship. It is best translated as an oath or pledge of allegiance made by a subject to hir sovereign. It also points out to us the modern problem of religious irrelevance.

WORSHIP: Reverent love and allegiance accorded to a sacred object and the rites by which this love and allegiance is expressed.
from: WOR-SHIP = WORTH = WEORTH
    = WER: to turn toward or opposite on the scales > to match
THUS to find or determine value or WORTH;
ALSO to turn into or become what one is worth
ALSO to be dependent on what befalls—fate or destiny
    (as a worth: that which befalls one)
ALSO allegiance: the act of turning toward
    the object of reverence or respect:
    directing attention toward or attending upon.
+ SHIP: the quality or condition of—;
the status, rank or office of—
    = SCHIPE = SCIPE = SKEP: to cut or hack (out) something, or
something cut out, SHAPE, SCOOP, SHAFT, SCAB, SCRAPE, SHAVE
THUS: (1) to determine the value or worth of something cut out
or by the cutting out of a specific shape, or
    (2) to turn toward a specific concept of something
        as the means of determining its worth, or
    (3) the turning toward (paying allegiance to) that
        specific concept separated from the milieu
        (cut out from the herd).

So what do YOU (WHO?) worship in your life? Let's try an experiment: since all scientists have open (?) minds and are receptive to ways of finding truth, our experiment ought to find reception in the reader. Those who are resistant to such experiment are, by definition, authoritarians who refuse to have logic or life lead their beliefs. Dear reader, which are you? WATCH IT!

Let us suppose that the four gospels are totally, in every way, a fake, a hoax, a fiction: it never happened. Our hypothetical experiment is to conceive that the four gospel writers (or others) got together and dreamed up the whole story for reasons irrelevant here. We make the assumption that the entirety (of the life of Jesus), from start to finish, is totally fictional.

In this frame of mind, now take this Bible and read the beatitudes from the Sermon on the Mount (Matthew 5:13) or any other of Jesus's sayings. Now, keeping our set firmly in mind, answer this question: do these beatitudes (or other citation) have any value? Do they, of themselves alone, say ANYTHING to you? Can you groove on the pure, naked truth—wherever and however it is found? Will you allow God to speak to you directly? The answer is to be found ONLY within you. So hold tight and WATCH IT!

*

Man's arrogance has been with him throughout the centuries. It invades every facet of hir life. One of the central parts of human life is politics: how one person relates to another and the ideas and attitudes s/he holds about hir collectivity. The perfect example is THE CHOSEN PEOPLE. Think about the arrogance of centuries of Hebrews depending upon such a belief. But before you slander them, remember that centuries of persecution forced the Jews to conclude that they were NOTOK. This "chosen people" thing gave them a WAY to cope with that. This is not merely an ancient problem, for Americans are tarred with the same brush: MANIFEST DESTINY. This new "chosen people" was singled out by God (?) to have, take, and use this fantastic frontier land and its resources. Instead of appreciating their luck (and God's gift) and having joy in it, they spent their energies coping with NOTOKness by proving that they were OK (and proving clearly, instead, their NOTOKness).

Such ignorance! God "out there" CHOSE these people (or this person) from among all the others. THAT is externalization, the shift of responsibility—the first sin: ARROGANCE, to arrogate authority to oneself, thus making oneself into a God. In such case, it was not God who made the choice of a people or of a person; it was the person himself who did the choosing—and s/he now refuses to admit it, refuses to take the responsibility for the decision. The Jews chose to be YHWH's people; that is internalization and submission.

The covenant of Abraham is, by definition, a two-party contract REQUIRING a CHOSEN consent on the part of the Hebrews. The people—all of those egos, identities, roles, personalities—by the simple presentation of a choice, were forced to choose, to accept, promise, agree to the deal or reject it.

The Constitution of the United States was once a covenant too. Starting with the Mayflower Covenant, the people of the then United States were, in 1787, presented with a choice. The mere presentation of the Constitution forced them to agree or disagree, and their choice was free. By 1861, those who had participated in the making of the commitment to the Constitution were dead. How many of the people, both North and South, had the opportunity to make their own free choice of Constitution (or constitutional provisions) at that time? Instead, what they CHOSE was to FORCE their WILLS on each other by war. They would NOT allow each other to have FREE CHOICE (being afraid of the result).

Is the political/economic/cultural/social system of the United States today the choice of anyone here, now, alive? Yes, new immigrants. But not natives. It isn't whether one is committed to or believes in the present Constitution (as interpreted); it is whether, in truth, one has had an opportunity to negate it. Thus, the Constitution and its usage has become, by the passage of time and nature, a status quo, which dominates and allows no choice and which resents the possibility of an option. The force involved in choice is a power made available by God/nature—clearly distinguishable from compulsion: the force of a collective, which is the denial of choice.

Well, then, DO we believe in a covenant of the people? If we do, then we MUST (i.e., it follows, inexorably) allow choice. If we do not allow choice, we MUST accept the TRUTH: that we do NOT believe in a covenant. (We look to our behavior in order to discover our beliefs.) A covenant provides the chance, the opportunity to promise, agree, accept or refuse, reject and deny. Does the status quo offer such a covenant to the people? If not, how can we expect this generation of Americans (are they such?) to have such a COMMITMENT to one another (social contract) that the forefathers had? Looking at the Declaration of Independence, we see that it was signed by those making the choice for themselves to commit their OWN "lives, fortunes, and sacred honor" to the cause.

Looking at this economic/cultural/social structure politically, we can see that we are denied certain alternative behaviorisms. If our range of response is curtailed, it is impossible to exercise response-ability (by definition, see page xxx). The result is a population thrown together without choice. Divisiveness is encouraged. The sense of duty to create and maintain a brotherly collective is discouraged. "Encourage" and "discourage" tell us of reinforcement theory. Our irresponsibility is reinforced positively and our responsibility is reinforced negatively. The reinforcements are backward.

Now, two groups (if it were only two) desire to control the United States: the so-called liberals and the so-called moralists. Both desire to dominate American life with their theories, attitudes, ideologies, sets, doctrines, and dogmas. In the process, they will dominate the people of this land: individual human BEINGS. Neither of these groups will allow, or even offer to allow, the freedom to the people to covenant together. Both wish to impose their own ideas on the people. The individuals in both of these groups demonstrate by their behavior that the control of their organisms lies in their identities. Clearly they stand for SLAVERY and against FREEDOM (Newspeak notwithstanding).

When individuals under the command of such limited capacity come together, thus multiplying their power, they create a power structure (the definition of "devil"). Although they are all authoritarians, they deny it and thus shift response-ability to the external God "out there." In so doing, they deny their own Christ-center, absolutely. We all pray that both sides will be unsuccessful. God may hear our prayer, but these groups will not. Their ideologies have failed, do fail, and will fail, for they are (by definition) NOT OF GOD; they are OF THIS WORLD, just as their emotions and intellects are under the control OF homo and not under the control OF that "more" MAN.

But they will not go away. The devil (see page xxx) is with us always—in each of us. Our identities strive to control the organism. We CANNOT—indeed, we MUST NOT—attempt to suppress (repress) our identities. That way is only another expression of our NOTOKness. Our identities must be seen and accepted for what they are. But as commanders of the organism, they are less than adequate; they are limited, infantile (also fragile, mortal). We must grow up, mature, accept the givens—the God-given reality—and choose surrender of the identity: command to the Christ-center so that truth might enter into the world.

As Paul said in his letter to the Ephesians, "For we wrestle not against flesh and blood, but against principalities, against powers, against the rulers of the darkness of this world, against spiritual wickedness in high places." The intellect at the top of the spine is the "high places" where the human ego and identity reigns. The ultimate corruption is the identity's insistence that it is NOT the devil, that it is NOT corrupt. Thus, being its own authority and denying it in the same breath: the shift of responsibility—the FIRST SIN. Mankind has been and will be beset by these enemies within hirself through all time, corrupting everything they touch.

Semantically, corruption is the putrefaction of the body—that mortal bushel basket of homo that covers the Christ-center within us. Thus, the usage of "corruption" is redundant: the body, organism, or identity IS mortal and corruptible—it perishes. To enshrine the doctrines, ideologies, and theories of the identity is the attempt to make a mortal thing—the identity—immortal. This is impossible, being a contradiction in terms. It cannot BE (exist). But the converse: the divine Christ-center-point of BEING is already enshrined in the temple of the organism. It need only have the devil step aside. But that requires a voluntary act based on conscious awareness.

Semantics is a tool most vital to man, for the corruption of language is the devil's most important tool. A simple quote from the Jesus people will suffice: "A study of the divinity of Jesus." Impossible! By definition, it is Christ who is divine. This is not a matter of belief; it is elementary. To raise the mortal identity to divine status is to enshrine the devil. What do they think Yeshuah came to tell us? We must WATCH for language corruption all around. The tool is to be eternally awake: WATCH IT!

*

The development and evolution of the Western world has not been (as is popularly supposed) from the CULTURAL (Old Europe, customs, religions, language) to the POLITICAL (independence, revolutions, constitutions), but rather the reverse: from POLITICS (Rousseau, Voltaire, Richelieu, Disraeli, Talleyrand, Machiavelli,

Bismarck, Churchill, and Clausewitz) to CULTURE (Jefferson, Hitler, fireside chats, industrialization, communism, bureaucracy, McDonald's). The apex of the shift was at the end of the Victorian era; the Great War announced the waning of the political age and the advent of the power of the cultural age.

> Western man has moved from government by X TO the holy princes of God's chosen church (to 1500); noble princes of the land led by God's chosen kings (1498– 1794); bourgeois princes of wealth: God's chosen moneyed people led by the robber barons (1776–1930); bureaucratic princes of knowledge—God's chosen educated:experts, specialists, scientists, managers (1930–200?), including computers and the information revolution.

Political age was based on Rousseau, Paine, and five revolutions. It means conscious words, intellect, ideas, ideologies culminating in the liberals' dependence on legislation and education. What happens when we shift from such political intellectual to the cultural? "Cultural" is based on UNCONSCIOUS motivations and drives, not words, but behavior (action). "From the political to the cultural" is a shift from conscious, intellectual, and overt ideologies to the study of man's subconscious, which is what actually drives his behavior.

Blacks have been freed by law and have had the opportunity to use legal freedom to its fullest. Nothing short of the institution of a new form of government can deny that. Now blacks are legislators to pass laws, judges to punish violators, bureaucrats to administer the laws, and educators to teach them; BUT the system is in the process of losing efficacy. The mores that control culture can't be legislated. Whites move out to the suburbs, Montana. We break nations, states, counties, cities apart. Resistance is part of the human soul. Whites will honor blacks legally but never in the depths of their soul. Whitey needs, emotionally and psychologically, an inferior to bolster hir unconscious conviction of hir own inferiority. A new form of government IS being instituted, based on "psychology is bullshit." Man is afraid to face hir inner self. It is a CULTURE of ILLUSION, FANTASY, and SCHIZOIDNESS.

FACTIONALISM: Specialization has led to every field separated from all the others; nonschool ideas are seen as heresy, requiring parties for advocacy purposes. Only the educated class will have the necessary savvy and income to form sufficiently powerful parties to force their will. The people are already the tools of bureaucratic propaganda.

Society will have to control the forces, people, and machines, or perish. The educated class is responding to this challenge and taking control through manning the bureaucracy—totalitarianism and dictatorship. The nobility of the scientist, expert, manager, "s/he who knows" is subverted by power, for power corrupts. This elite (like all others before it) will do whatever it has a mind to do. CATCH 22! (They can do anything they can get away with.)

Freedom and response-ability for the individual demands that s/he have the fullest possible range of response available to hir. To be constrained and inhibited by law, legislation, unconscious community mores, etc., is to lack freedom. This denies responsibility to the people. To set up such a system and then complain about these consequences is ridiculous. But closer analysis points out that it is the way for rulers to create serfdom and, at the same time, absolve themselves of the guilt for the consequences of their acts.

The elite are able to communicate in meaningful ways among themselves, but the common man has not been taught to read analytically and critically. The elite control the media (propaganda) and indulge the people in their consumer whims while taking their birthright (freedom and the response-ability to exercise it) from them. The common man no longer has effective ways to deal or cope with, in or against this so-necessary control. Control of the propaganda media, being in this minority educated class leads to unemployment (now titled leisure), which leads to apathy, indolence, indulgence, decadence, impotence, alienation, anxiety, and crime.

The cure (if any) is in the concept of cybernetics—KYBERNETES: to steer, pilot > govern, steersman, governor: the control of one's OWN behavior. Democracy, any kind of self-government, begins with one's government of Self, actualized and realized. Control of human behavior lies with the Spirit, GOD, the Christ-center. Humans must learn to be awake and aware. It is the natural outgrowth (next step) of the shift from political (left-brained, conscious, intellectual, verbal) to cultural (right-brained, unconscious, understanding, action).

CHAPTER XII

PATRIARCHY VS. CAREER

HOLLAND'S HEX: Results Orientation
(From Strong Business Personality Inventory Test)

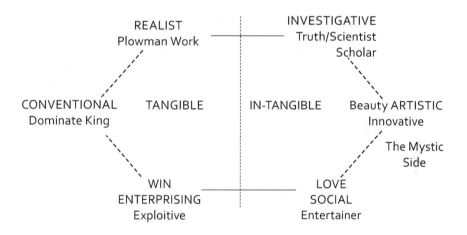

The left side of the hex is the patriarchal side, centered on the C personality. Patriarchy is not distinguishable from matriarchy, for their attitudes are parallel, differing only in gender emphasis. A patriarch has one central purpose (whether conscious or unconscious, effective or relatively ineffective, hidden or exposed) and that is to PRODUCE, MAINTAIN, PROMOTE, and EXPAND (PMPE) (to varying degrees) income, status, estate, holdings, power, influence—all these pragmatic things—for one central reason: for the benefits of and for hir family fortunes (FF). "Family" includes the extended family and retainers, "not of the blood" but who have been of service: the classic meanings of servants, son and Pater.

The patriarch does not focus on raising hir status in society (i.e., being upwardly mobile). These are only means to the true end: PMPE-FF. As s/he is successful, s/he does expect to be made president, etc. The definition of "presbyter" is rule by the elders of a community, congregation, or other association—ruled by those who have proved themselves to be effective patriarchs in PMPE, their own FF. S/he knows that the most effective patriarchs will be recognized by other patriarchs and given the greater responsibilities. This is the elemental basis for democracy. Democracy, as defined by patriarchs, is not extended to any of their servants or retainers. The American Constitution recognized this by using a "landowners" test for voting qualification. And, of course, any reform must be passed through the hands (not the minds) of the elders, the ruling status quo.

The final responsibility of the patriarch is to replace himself with one of the younger generation—but one who has proved himself more relevant to the changing times than the older patriarch. Only when the older can see clearly that the younger is effectively and productively more relevant than the older will s/he accept that it is hir responsibility to hand over the reins. Thus, the hidden purpose— future PMPE of the F-amily F-ortune—is paramount. All is sacrificed to that end, including being the paramount patriarch, when it is necessary to the PMPE-FF: income, holdings, estate, status, power, influence. Since to the Patriarch there is only one possible goal in anybody's life, s/he accepts hir son/daughter, or rejects hir, solely on hir calculation, assessment, prediction, conscious or unconscious, of the hir capability in PMPE-FF.

"Ambition" is a word that actually does not fit herein, being more appropriate to "career." But to a patriarch, it means that degree of expansion (beyond mere maintenance), which the individual conceives as possible and to which s/he dedicates himself. But the only career envisioned here is the game, folly, vanity, effort to PMPE: produce, maintain, promote, and expand -FF. The business, investments, enterprise, field, profession, or pursuit are only and always the means to the end. "Career" being an end in itself, the patriarch is thus never engaged in a career.

To the patriarch, the truth is what s/he says it is—there can be no external truth. S/he attempts to be correct; however, "correctness" has the limited definition: that which is effective in PMPE-FF. Thus, that the world is spherical is unimportant since it is irrelevant; hir life is lived here and now on this flat-appearing earth. If s/he is genial, open, and giving enough, s/he will ask the scientist for the relevance of this spherical earth truth (and its relevance to hir unspoken goal: PMPE-FF).

Ideas, principles, and ideals are all intangible and involve a lot of time and attention to study, thinking, and talk—all a waste of the little time one has to give to PMPE-FF. Reform of the known evils of society is denied for one very central reason: the patriarch has invested a lifetime in learning how the culture operates and how to PMPE for the FF within that culture. To change it makes hir knowledge irrelevant, and s/he would become a failure. Change occurs fast enough as it is. Anyone (including hir own beloved son) who makes efforts to change the parameters of that culture is hir enemy; anything that works against hir PMPE-FF is hir enemy. In like manner, s/he looks for people to aid in hir effort, but s/he judges them solely from the standpoint of their aid in PMPE for hir -FF. Career thinking on their part signals clearly to hir that, being independent, they are not trustworthy. Besides, "career" entails so much risk from which little PMPE for the FF can be predicted.

"Career" is a word exclusive to the right side of the hex, having to do with development of self. The right side is, by definition, searching for intangible results. But there are no intangible results that are of benefit to the family. Truth, beauty, and love are all personal acquisitions; the patriarch sees them as irrelevant and selfish. And in hir dominating control, s/he sees hirself as the most sacrificing, never being interested in self at all—only PMPE of F-amily F. Career employees are hired only as need be. The patriarch refuses to learn what is needed hirself, but when the need for knowledge and information is seen, s/he HIRES servants and retainers and exploits them as s/he is able. If they serve hir PMPE-FF, hir patriarchal purpose, s/he will repay them. A patriarch does not grant raises to retainers; however, s/he takes care of them and their relatives old age at a later date. But the employee who demands a rightful raise is seen as enemy (inhibiting the expansion of the FAMILY fortunes), thus, someone to exploit and therefore expendable: s/he owes such independence nothing. (If that employee has the economic power to demand that raise, that releases the padron from further responsibility toward hir: s/he is no longer a retainer; s/he is now an independent contractor.)

Which points out that hir relationship to the external world is contractual. If they are willing to serve HIR PMPE-FF, s/he will reciprocate in helping them, in THEIR PMPE-FF, BUT NOT FOR THEIR CAREER. Hir relationship to hir spouse is also contractual (whether conscious or subliminal). And since s/he is on a one-dimensional trip (patriarchy), s/he does not talk, think, or contemplate hir relationships. Marriage requires a contemplation only of whether this spouse will be effectively a benefit (or conversely a loss) to hir PMPE-FF goal. Later divorce, then, can only be seen as an admission that s/he is a poor patriarch since s/he made an earlier mistake.

Hir relationship to God is as one inferior patriarch to another superior one. (One patriarch recognizes another.) And hir general prayer is ever: help my PMPE-FF (not me). S/he understands Jehovah, the authoritarian patriarchal God ever interested in hir special chosen people (retainers, family) for whom s/he cares lovingly. Thus, hir world has only hir one dimensionality.

In order for any staff person to emphasize the intangibles of the right side of the hex in hir life, s/he must somehow have hir tangible necessities supplied to hir BY SOMEONE ELSE: WHO, of necessity, IS A PATRIARCH. It is best seen as a "protection racket." The careerist hired by a corporation is being paid from the profits produced (PMPE) by patriarchs. And s/he is then, by definition, a retainer—no longer independent.

Of course, there are smarter, quicker, more intuitive, more aggressive, more enterprising, thus more successful patriarchs. Thus inherent to this way is the acceptance that there will be losers: unsuccessful patriarchs. But that is acceptable on a genetic basis: unsuccessful—elements of any animal life breed less than successful ones, thus improving the genetic heritage of survivors. Genetic success is equivalent to patriarchal success. Thus, the demise of losers is not only acceptable, but desirable. Thus, the death penalty makes good sense to patriarchs (including that of hir beloved son).

As in all human relations, patriarchy can be misused, abused, and become corrupted—and does exactly so. We normally refer to the status quo as bad, evil, inappropriate, or counterproductive. And, indeed, abused patriarchy occurs when the patriarch refuses to turn over governance to the younger when the younger has been adequately trained and proved hir competence, recognizing that newer understandings are more relevant to modern times than the older. This occurs when a generation of patriarchs has forgotten their responsibility to their own PMPE-FF and has become selfish, frightened, or greedy. When such corruption becomes prevalent in the culture, the young are left with no alternative to taking their own patriarchal position by force. That revolution breeds hate and fear and is, in itself, counterproductive: all caused by an existing status quo patriarchy that has corrupted itself.

One normal cause of patriarchal corruption is affluence: the patriarch has been exceedingly successful. S/he has exceeded hir own ambitions sufficiently that s/he cannot see any necessity in further expansion of the FF (i.e., there is nothing for the son to do but enjoy the proceeds). Since the environment is always in a state of continual change, s/he is wrong. Hir observations should make it evident that this is a period when the future will demand what s/he cannot envision; thus, s/he must turn over governance to someone quite different from hirself. But s/he is subverted from hir duties to the PMPE-FF by hir own feelings of self-satisfaction. The enemy is affluence. When men are hungry, they never make these mistakes, individually or en mass.

When a status quo takes control over the state for self-protective purposes, it is their own children that they see as their enemy instead of as their replacements. They tie their children's hands out of fear of loss of their relative affluence and status. They promulgate security measures to protect themSELVES: selfishness to the detriment of their own children. They have lost their positive focus on the PMPE for FF and shifted to negative self-protective attitudes designed to eliminate fear, risk, and dynamism. At its core they—once patricians, now tyrants (dictators)—deny patriarchy (their heritage) to their own children.

And they, now abandoning patriarchy, hire only employees, careerists, to whom they have no responsibility other than the overt, conscious contract or regulatory code. What, in reality, actually is their employee's fate is not their business; they no longer have retainers, they no longer have a family, they have become autocrats—dictators.

Seeing patriarchy, per se, as evil is incorrect. Matriarchy can also be corrupted. It is the corruption that is evil—immorality that must be confronted. Careerism is an appropriate approach for the young, but we must see that it is the very insidiousness of careerism that kills the independence of the young. Only independence can make a successful patriarch. Yet the modern economy only allows for a very few patriarchs and very many careerists. A careerist is one who learns (well) a speciality and can fill a narrow need envisioned by a patriarch: a corporate (read socialist-bureaucrat) slot. There are almost no possible opportunities for the masses to engage in PMPE of their FF. Thus, generation after generation, the number of slots for careerists and dependent employees expand, and the number of effective, responsible, successful patriarchs diminishes. And, in addition, the class of welfare serfs expands—little by little killing the great experiment of American independence, democracy, and liberty.

It is the decline of the gentility and the rise of the MASS SOCIETY of irresponsible consumers. No one can lead the homogenous mass of careerist specialists as they strive (upward mobility) for more money by cheating and exploiting each other. Thus, open government falls to the hidden smoke-filled rooms of contracting enterprisers, attaining power and money through politics.

The age of patriarchs, which began nine thousand years ago, is coming to an end. The great sea of change that has occurred, which makes ALL the difference, is conscious AWARENESS. Now people know and, through study, can perceive patriarchy as their dominant existential medium.

The central essence of patriarchy as it exists in the unconscious mind of its practitioners is JEHOVAH.

JEHOVAH AND PATRIARCHY

The ultimate patriarch is Jehovah. The Bible is true because he said it was. No amount of study, research, archeology, etc., can allow the scientist to look at the patriarch's product critically. If s/

he is allowed to do so, then the truth is no longer patriarchal. Look at the Ten Commandments. Each is so worded as to be ambiguous. We must kill in order to live but the commandment says no killing. Since it is clear that the commandment is wrong, useless, irrelevant, thus to be ignored, it follows that the Lord who gave those rules is also irrelevant, to be ignored. But then the truth would no longer be handed down by rule (-archy) of the father-god (patri-).

How did this happen? Originally, in the Hebrew religion, the topmost god was the unspeakable tetragrammaton: YHWH. What that symbolized is translated by the King James Version as "I AM THAT I AM," and the Greek "ON" translated to "being." Thus, the top of the cosmological hierarchy was an existential acceptance of the essence of being and suchness (very nurturingly feminine, but not matriarchal).

But at a later date, the vowels from ELOHIM and ADONAI were added to make YeHoVah (W=V), or Jehovah, who was now the top father-god image: patriarch. The god no longer was a here-and-now experience of reality, but an externalized supervisory Lord: a god of power. That shift is of the greatest order, for it was the work of Master Jesus, KRISDHAZ, to shift it back again. He pointed to his own name as THEWAY: Yeshuah, which was spelled in the ancient mystical script YHSWH, or YH S WH. The *S* was the symbol for "on earth" or "here and now." Thus, his name meant "BEING HERE AND NOW; I AM THAT I AM ON EARTH."

No matter how one translates these words, it becomes clear that the Master was shifting from a patriarchal god to a god of love active here and now in each of us; from an externalized power to an internalized BEING: the father (patriarch) within and the kingdom of heaven within.

Thus, the Master's truth exposes patriarchy as THE OPPRESSOR, which the Redeemer came to SAVE MAN FROM. It is a shift from cultural power orientation to the recognition, perception, and awareness of man's true place in the world. Thus, the recognizer, perceiver (SEER: see-er), the one aware and awake is the enemy of the patriarchy. JEHOVAH then is the FIRST and PRIMARY foundation of patriarchy. And Master Yeshuah, Krisdhaz, brought us THEWAY to save ourselves from that patriarchy: its God, the social power structure, the bosses, or our own parent.

He taught us of the father within or of the existence of our own inner patriarch, which obviated the need for external patriarchy. One could conclude that Jesus had picked this PARENT image from transactional analysis.

*

I LIVE IN A DEPRESSING ENVIRONMENT:
WHAT CAN I DO ABOUT IT?

Stop looking at it as depressing;
Bless every aspect and facet of it;
Pray and bless those who use me despitefully;
Make peace with it; free consciousness from concentration on it
Put no psychic energy or attention on it,
    THUS, no disappointment, resentment, frustration can occur.
"Depression" merely is an allocation of
justification/rationalization for action.
The true reason is an inner desire for change.
I call it "depressing."
The environment may or may not be depressing,
but remaining in it when one doesn't want to be there
is itself depressing = I am depressing myself.
The cure is to get out of the depressing environment.
    NO! FIRST, make primary that inner desire for freedom.
THUS, I can ask, what problem do I seek to solve by flight?

HOW CAN I, ONLY AN INFANT, DEAL WITH
THE DREADFUL AND TERRORIZING POWER OF FATHER-GOD?
BUT I am no longer an infant;
I am a fully potent man of experience and knowledge.
IF I have trouble loving my opponents: it is because I am biased.
That is, I project my repressed feelings (biases)
on others and the environment.
I repress my feelings because I learned to do that as a child.
I repressed (swallowed) my fears, anxieties, awe, and dread of
    my father because I did not have the power to cope with it.
I was, in fact, dependent for survival on his good will.

But today's authorities are not my father; I am not an infant.
YET I feel that I am personally dependent on all those
whose authoritative stance reminds me of him.
But I am NOT dependent on others: I am free   —   YAM FREE.
Others who abuse me—use me despitefully—
are projecting their own repressed feelings on me.
They, like I, are in a straitjacket in which
they feel dependent on me for rescue of some sort.
I now set free all who would impose upon me the bondage
      of enmity, prejudice, or unfair criticism,
no longer responding to them as if they were my parent.
Start looking for God (attend to—stretch for the NEUMENON)
instead of staring at the problem.
I give power to appearances, PHENOMENA, by believing in them.
I reverse this by asserting that the APPEARANCE, PHENOMENON,
is not the truth; the NEUMENON is always the truth.
This is faith rather than logic.
I do not deny facts (PHENOMENA), rather I transcend them by
proclaiming a higher truth (reaching toward the NEUMENON).
If I look at what I am afraid of until I really understand it,
it will no longer have any fear for me.
No issue in human affairs can be resolved if those involved
refuse to confront one another
and the issue itself with self-honesty.
My fears remain unresolved because I am dishonest about them.
Withdrawal is a failure to confront.
      When people hurt me, instead of confronting them with it,
I nurse my wounds (take care of myself) and withdraw.
I am afraid of further hurt if I approach them,
or I am afraid that I cannot trust my own responses.
But I cannot be healed of a fear if I refuse to face it.
It is miserable to be running scared.
I must have the spiritual integrity (to myself)
to refuse absolutely to let this happen to me.
There are issues I must deal with, and I WILL to do so.
Because I am honest, I will have the help of God.
Those who have great faith have great power.
Deep in the core (genes) of the acorn are the instructions

(DNA) of how to make a successful oak tree.
Likewise, deep at the center (core = heart) of man (me)
are all the instructions for what I am: BHE—
the fullness of this expression of God
and how to achieve that.
THERE IS MY ACHIEVEMENT GOAL.

In deciding what I shall say and do and what I shall NOT
    say and do, I am functioning at a creative level,
whether I am aware of it or not.
Such decisions determine some part of the environment,
and I choose behaviors relevant to that determination.
This is the process that establishes what my environment is.
I identify with that which haunts me, not to fight it off,
but to take it into myself;
it represents rejected elements in me.
The shadow side of the self, which is denied (repressed),
represents the ANIMA (Lat.): soul, spirit.
"Animus" means both a feeling of hostility,
a violent, malevolent intention (animosity)
AND to animate: to give spirit to, to enliven.
The denied part is the source of hostility and aggression, but when,
through consciousness, I integrate it into my self-system,
    it becomes the source of energy and spirit, which enlivens me.
I must incorporate the daimonic
because it will possess me if I don't.
The one way to get over daimonic possession is to possess it,
    by confronting it, coming to terms with it, integrating it.
This process yields several benefits: it
    strengthens the self by integrating what has been left out;
    overcomes the "split" schizoidness,
that paralyzing ambivalence in the self;
    renders the person more "human" by breaking down
self-righteousness and aloof detachment,
the usual defense of he who denies the daimonic.
Males are freed from morbid ties to the past and mother-ties.
    The female is seen as daimonic because every individual,
male or female, begins life with ties to the mother.

This biological imbeddedness to "mother" is an attachment
    that the human being must fight in order to develop
his own consciousness and autonomy of action
    —if he is to possess himself.
But having fought, won, and thus able to declare his autonomy,
he must welcome the daimonic back on a conscious plane.
Overcoming passive dependency on mother,
one is able to assert himself.
Working on a problem of will—the inability to assert oneself
to authority—one gains the ability to love with great abandon.

CHAPTER XIII

We must distinguish the powers and principalities OF the world from the KINGDOM of GOD:

KINGDOM= KING + DOM = from the PIE roots GENE + DHE

GENE: to give birth, beget—extended to various aspects and results of procreation, and thus to familial and tribal groups. (NOTE: in the ancient root language the sound represented by *H, G, GH, K* were all a guttural GKH, as in HASIDIM (Heb.), GILA (Sp.). It was made harsher or softened as it evolved and was represented by differing letters.)

GENE = GNYO = KUNJAM (Teut.): family, race = CYNN (Old Eng.), KIN
    = KUNINGAZ (Teut.): son (not daughter) of the royal kin
    = CYNING (Old Eng.) = KING
    = KUN: kin, clan, family, tribe + ING + AZ: s/he who or that which
    1. ING makes nouns out of verbs
    2. ING indicates the possession of certain quality, nature
      = possesses those qualities of the KUN: clan, tribe, etc.
THUS, best personifies tribal qualities;
    3. ING indicates the act, process, or art
      of performing the verb act = coitus by the king;
    4. ING indicates something necessary for the verb act
      to take place = the King and a female;
    5. ING indicates that which is the result of the verb act:
THUS, he begets a KING;
    6. ING indicates belonging to, connected with,
      or having the character of the verb act,
      its consequences, qualities, etc.;

7. ING indicates that which accomplishes such an action:
    the KUN is he who begets the kin of a clan
    = he is the ALPHA MALE
THUS he is the dominant sire of tribal kin
THUS, KING = KUN-ING-AZ: the alpha male, the dominant sire
of all tribal kin, who best personifies those qualities,
which the tribe considers most proper and valuable.
KING = CYNG = CYNING = KUNING = KUN-ING-AZ; KUN = GN = GENE
GENE = GN-TI = KUNDJAZ (Teut.) = CYND (Old Eng.):
origin, race, family = KIND
    = KUNDIZ (Teut.): natural, native
    = CYNDE: fitting = KIND
    = KINTH (Teut.) = KIND (Ger.): child; (KITH)
    = GENS (Lat.): race, clan
    = GENTILE, GENTLE (gentleman)
    = GEN-ES = GENUS (Lat.): race, kind
    = GENDER, GENERATE, GENEROUS, GENRE
    = GENOS (Grk.): race, family
    = GEN-YO = GENIUS (Lat.): creative divinity,
       inner spirit, innate quality
    = INGENIUM (Lat.): inborn character = INGENIOUS
    = GEN-A = INDIGENA (Lat.): born in a place = INDIGENOUS
    = GEN-WO = INGENUUS (Lat.): native, natural, freeborn
    = GEN-MEN = GERMEN (Lat.): shoot, bud, embryo, GERM
    = GENA-TI = GENESIS (Grk.): birth, beginning
    = GENESIS: origins
    = GI-GN = GIGNERE (Lat.): to beget = GENITAL, PROGENY
    = GIGNESTHAI (Grk.): to be born = EPIGENE
    = GN-O = BENI: good + GNUS (Lat.): good-natured, kindly
    = BENIGN
    = GNA = PRAEGNAS (Lat.): before birth = PREGNANT
    = GNA-SKO = GNASCI > NASCI (Lat.): to be born
    = NASCENT, NATIVE, NATURE, COGNATE, INNATE, NATION
    = GON-O = GONOS (Grk.): child, procreation, seed = GONAD
    = GEN = ZADAN (Persian): to be born
    = ZATA (Persian): born, free
    = GN = JA (Sanskrit): born, produced, originated

All of these roots reinforce the several central thoughts:

1. Kin, family, clan, tribe, kind, race
2. Born, beget, procreation, beginning, child
3. Native, natural, fitting
4. Character, spirit, quality: freeborn, good-natured, kindly, gentle, generous, even divinity

THUS, A KING is he who is most fitting to beget the children and make up the tribe that is, in fact, of a kind. He thus begets kings, and thus, all members of the tribe are kings. He best personifies those qualities of spirit and character that the tribe (the constituency) finds most proper and valuable; namely, good-natured, kindly, gentle, generous, free, and even divine. This is why they make him king and why they maintain him in that office. Yes, he is a most powerful patriarch; that is one of the things the tribe values—but only one.

THUS, KING = the dominant sire of all tribal kin who best personifies those qualities the tribe considers most proper and valuable.

+ -DOM = DHE: to set, put, THUS establish
 = DHO = DON (Teut.) = DON (Old Eng.): to do = DO
 = DHE-TI: thing laid down or done = DEDIZ (Teut.)
 = DAED (Old Eng.): a doing = DEED
 = DHO-MO = DOMAZ (Teut.): thing set or put down
 = DOM (Old Eng.): judgment = DOOM
 = -DOM: state, condition, or power
 = -DOMR (Old Norse): condition
 = DOMS (Gothic): judgment = DUMA
 = DOMJAN (Teut.) = DEMAN (Old Eng.): to judge = DEEM
THUS, -DOM: the state or condition of things:
the existing situation, status quo
 = DHOT = DOS (Lat.): doer, performer
 = SACERDOS: performer of sacred rites, priest
 = DHE = KOM-DHE: to put together
 = CONDERE (Lat.): establish, preserve = CONDIMENT
 = KRE-DHE: place trust = CREDERE (Lat.): to believe
 = CREDIT, CREDO, CREDIBLE, CREDULOUS
 = DHE-K = FACERE (Lat.): to do, make = FACT, FEATURE,

AFFECT, EDIFY, PERFECT, PROFIT, SURFEIT
= FACIES (Lat.): form, shape (form imposed on
   something) = FACE, FAÇADE, DEFACE, SURFACE
= OP-FICI-OM (Lat.): performance of OP: work
= OFFICIUM: service, duty, business = OFFICE
= DHE-K-OLI = FACILIS (Lat.): feasible, easy
= FACULTY, FACILITY, DIFFICULTY
= DHI-DHE = TITHENAI (Grk.): to put = THESIS
= DHE-MN = THEMA (Grk.): thing placed, proposition = THEME
= DHE-TLO = DATLOS (Celtic): a putting together
= DAL: assembly
= DHE-DHE = DADHATI (Sanskrit): s/he places = SANDHI
= DH = AWIS-DH-IO = AW: to perceive + DH = AWDHIO
= AUDIRE (Lat.): to hear = AUDIO, AUDIENCE, AUDIT
= OB-AWIS-DHE = OBEY (see page xxx)

KING = the dominant sire of all tribal kin who best personifies those qualities the tribe considers most proper and valuable. PLUS -DOM: the state or condition of things—the existing situation, status quo.

THUS, KINGDOM = the state, condition, system, or status quo that personifies those qualities the tribe considers most proper and valuable—established, executed, and maintained by the power of the dominant alpha males of the tribe.

All tribal values and qualities are created by natural selection and unconsciously continued by the traditional behavior and practice of the tribe.

The king is maintained by the tribe so long as he continues those qualities and personifies them. As his power wanes with age, his tenure depends on the projections of repressed hate by the tribe based on his previous conduct: how close to the traditional tribal values he hewed. If he truly personified those values, he will be maintained long out of respect. But tyrants fall early.

A KING is he who is most fitting to father the tribal children. The tribe (the constituency) finds most proper and valuable those qualities of spirit and character; namely, good-natured, kind, gentle, generous, free, and even divinity. Yes, they also value power (power defends the tribe), but it is only one of their values.

KINGDOM OF GOD: That god (see page xxx) who is most fitting to FATHER the children of the tribe will be the tribal god. He is fitting so long as the tribe finds him possessing and projecting those qualities they most highly value.

This applies also to the modern Christian divinity in this scientific age. This traditional "god" no longer sufficiently personifies tribal values. And present urban values are just as unconsciously held and projected. Today's conflict is between modern urban and traditional agrarian values. The liberals are urban, and the conservatives are regressing nostalgically and hopefully to older obsolete [* infra] values. The "consciousness revolution" is merely the effort to bring all of these conflicting values out of the unconscious into the light of day and the open air in defiance of the denial taboo.

[*] OBSOLETE because the US is irredeemably now since (1911–1947 = 1929 +– 20 years), a predominately urban nation and absolutely no longer agrarian; and since 1978+– over thirty years primarily suburban.

In the midst of this conflict, those on both sides see the other as the ABOMINATION OF DESOLATION (Matthew 24:15); Mark 13:14 states, "But when ye therefore shall see the abomination of desolation, spoken of by Daniel the prophet [Daniel 11:31], standing in the holy place where it ought not [whoso (let him that) readeth, let him understand:], then... flee into the mountains."

ABOMINATION: to detest or abhor, great dislike or loathing
    from ABOMINARI (Lat.): to shun as a bad omen
    = AB: away from + OMEN: portend, presage, a prognostic sign
THUS, ABOMEN = a negative OMEN:
    that which signifies evil, bad, loathing, etc.
    from O: to announce, to hold as true
    + MEN: to think, states of mind and thought; mind,
mindful, mental, memory, remember, recall, recollect, remind, warn, advise, counsel, prayer, hymn, wisdom—willing, mad, madness, mania, spirit, love
ALSO project, projecting points, jut out
    > threaten, mountain
ALSO remain, mansion

ALSO isolated, rare, alone, single, only, sole
An OMEN, as we know, does not have meaning extraneous to what one projects on the event. Thus, there must be an external event and a wise autonomous (single, projecting) person who REMEMBERS from hir spirit—MANIA, MIND, MEMORY—what that event (OMEN) portends and announces (O) it to hir audience (AUDIO: those who hear) = that is an OMEN.

And an ABOMEN is an event, a phenomena, that, to one who thinks for hirself and controls hir projections from an attentive memory, has the negative meanings of terror, bad, or evil consequences.

THUS, when you apprehend
the inner negative meaning of such bad OMEN—
of DESOLATION: devoid of inhabitants, deserted,
unfit for habitation by any life; forsaken, abandoned
from DESOLARE: abandon = DE: completely + SOLUS: alone
from SEU: self, own's own, relative, SIBLING, SUI-, SOLO
    = SWEDH: that which is one's own
      (land, peculiarity, custom, color, mores)
    = SWEDH-NO = ETHNOS (Grk.): people of one's own kind
    = band of people living together = a nation, people
    = SWO = SVA (Sanskrit) own's own master = SWAMI, prince
THUS, SOLATION is the place absent of your kind, kin, friends, people, allies, AND
DE: completely so.

THUS, when you perceive that negative or bad OMEN that presages or portends the complete wasting, ruin, and desolation of a place (Brazilian rainforest), making it unfit for habitation by, and thus the abandonment of it by your own kind, people, friends, allies (chernoble);

THUS, when you apprehend the meaning of that negative bad omen signaling such complete desolation of a place as to render it unfit for habitation by your own kind—

standing in the HOLY place—
HOLY: sacred, revered from HALIG (Old Eng.)
    = KAILO (PIE): whole, uninjured, healthy, of good omen
    = HEALed, HALLOWed: to bless
THUS, the hallowed place that is healthy, whole, uninjured,
where it doesn't belong.

THUS, when you see that bad OMEN signaling such complete
desolation of a place as to render it unfit for habitation by your own
kind standing in that most holy, hallowed, blessed, healthy, whole,
uninjured place;

THUS, when you perceive that bad omen signaling such complete
desolation of a place as to render it totally unfit for habitation by your
own KIND, standing in the most HOLY place—

then HEAD FOR THE HILLS, the dam has bust!

KIND (see king supra): 1. Kin, family, clan, tribe, race;
    2. Born, beget, beginning, child;
    3. Native, natural, fitting;
    4. Character, spirit: free, gentle,
Generous, even divinity.

If we assume the most natural and fitting in the human is a free,
gentle, and generous character or spirit, then that is the Holy Ghost,
the Christ-center.

THUS, when you perceive that bad OMEN signaling such total
desolation of the human in BHEING to be no longer fit for habitation
by the Christ-center/Spirit-God, then flee to the mountains.

MOUNTAIN = MONS (Lat.): mountain from MEN (PIE): see above OMEN
THUS, Mount Meru and the CENTER of your own BHEing.

FINALLY, when YOU perceive and understand from that negative bad
omen signaling such total desolation of the human BHEing and hir

environment that it is no longer fit for habitation by the Christ-center (God), then YOU flee to Mount Meru and hold firmly to it NOW!

*

MOUNT MERU is the mountain at the center of the earth from which top man can see everything—that is, hir consciousness is expanded to include the entire world, that s/he has unified with God and is hirself OMNI-present, -scient, -potent. It is the place where s/he erects hir Shushumna into the cosmos, centers hirself, drops off the baggage (identity), and enters hir closet. If those who think they see the abomination of desolation were to follow this advice, the rest of us would have nothing to fear from them and only good to expect. But instead, we are surrounded by powers and principalities who expect us to just like them (catch 22). But we (WHO?) must never surrender to THEM. Instead, we must turn away from the world and climb Mount Meru ourselves. The more who do so, the more the ABOMEN is proven wrong. But I need not tell you (WHO?) that (see Jonah).

CHAPTER XIV

Let us now turn forward and cease analysis of the past. What can the individual do about these things? First, s/he must apprehend the semantic and linguistic meaning of "individual" (WHO?). Secondly, s/he can begin to realize the implications of these truths. S/he is pointing to the organism when s/he speaks of the individual, and s/he is asking, "What can the identity do?" S/he certainly isn't asking, "What can God do?" God is and WILL "DO" on his own agenda. If all men are OK and the only problem that any of us have is with ourSelves, then all there is to do is to PRAISE, LOVE, and THANK God. And that we have been told for millennia—and rejected it.

But look at those words! They are ridiculous and meaningless as mere words. What concepts do they symbolize? Since the divine center is the Christ within us, then let us actualize IT, realize IT, make it happen. WHO? HOW? Simply (?) follow the instructions you have already been given. First, enter your closet. Second, sit right down in the middle of yourSelf. Third, quiet your identity. Fourth, Watch IT! This is called centering yourself, or meditation. Meditate, find your center, lift off that bushel basket, and allow IT to command the organism: the actualization of the TRUE SELF. There is ONLY this ONEWAY.

Enter the tabernacle of the Lord, and Tabernacle with the Lord—a TABERNACLE was the hut, inn, tent used as a portable sacred temple or sanctuary by the Hebrews. As a verb, it means to dwell temporarily (to dwell in a temporary tent)—from TABERNACULUM (Lat.): tent the diminutive of TABERNA (Lat.): hut or inn:

a public house open to travelers: TAVERN.

THUS, the sacred temple or sanctuary within the mind, body, or self, which is a portable temple carried along with the traveler on the way that is always available to enter to meet with God.
THUS, TO TABERNACLE with God is to
    STOP externality, center oneself;
    ENTER your closet, keep the silence; and
    OBEY: OB-AU-DHE—hear, listen (see page xxx).

And when you (the organism) have become (not made) a conduit for God, then you will have provided the greatest gift to the world that you have the ability to bestow. And you (WHO?) achieve this by getting out of the WAY, yielding the command from and by you to the center. WATCH IT! How? You (your identity) don't know how, but your body does. You have already been told.

If you insist on giving that identity an education, then study Zen, Sufi, Tao, the Kabbalah, Tarot, the gospels, donJuan, or many, many more. Remember that NONE of them are THEWAY, and ALL of them are THEWAY. In all efforts, stay awake, meditate, contemplate, and WATCH what you read, what you see, what you experience, how you respond, what you actually DO, how you feel, and what you conceive or think. There are many paths to discovery. Some will fit better than others; some will not feel right at all. Take the response-ability to WATCH over your own organism and discover. Krishnamurti: Be totally aware and make no effort.

Your organism? "Your" is the possessive form indicating that "you" possess, have, own the organism. For that, it follows that "you" and the organism MUST be entirely separate. Try this little test, follow these instructions: (1) read these instructions first; (2) hold your hand in front of our face and look at it; (3) as you gaze at your hand, answer this question: "Whose hand is that?" Certainly you answered, "Mine." "Mine" is also the possessive form. Thus, "it" belongs to "me." WHO? Your own words indicate the separation and the resultant alienation of this entity who answers from the organism. You are not at fault; you merely have been asleep. Recognize the truth inherent in your own mouth. Let this TRUTH sink in if you must sit and look at your hand all month.

It is true that "you" SIT in the driver's seat of this body. That is a very apt metaphor and more true than we have allowed. If you consider the Christ-center as the true entity of life, then it resides IN this organism. WHY? Because the center REQUIRES a body in order to adapt to the environment. The body has the means of (a) refueling itself, (b) receptive organs to pass information into the central processor, (c) an adaptive filter system for the capture of oxygen and the discharge of wastes, and (d) tools for the manipulation of the environment at the WILL of the driver. This body is the life-support system for the "center"—it is its space suit. Thus, this local representative of God is enabled to adapt to this hostile environment and survive while it carries out its master's mission.

So WHO? is driving this space suit? The identity is the illusion of identification with the space suit, a convenient figment of the central processor conjured up as a ruling center by the organism—which is the mere housing for WHO? Whatever the entity within, it is there to command the life-support system; it only exists for the design purposes of its creator.

That body, that organism, has been in existence since the beginning of time: it is eternal. Is that arrogance? No, this body of mine has been around since the world began, at least. It is made up of atoms that have not been just created; they have been here all the time. The atoms of my body are continually changing, but those that are gathered here now from the environment to replace the old are not newly created atoms (or molecules); they are only in a new form. There are no "new" atoms on earth. Since the formation of the earth, all the earth's atoms have been reworked and reformed by the cosmic forces at work on her.

Why should these atoms come together to make up this body? There is an organizing force, an energy field, present that causes these atoms to line up in their specific patterns that constitute this body. What is that force? Since we do not know with our materialistic minds what energy is or about energy flows, it is, therefore, unknown to us. But we use metaphors to indicate, point to, label that force: "the spark of life," the "Christ-centerpoint"—God's energy entering into the organism though that center. This is the power that creates, maintains, and drives this organism. This is the energy flow that causes us such awe—even overawe.

You (your organism) are created by God. Thus, you are OK, acceptable, perfect. Where you are RIGHT NOW is where you are supposed to be—the place where you have been put by God; it is an OK place. You already are in the middle of yourSelf. You need only become AWARE of that truth. Where you find yourSelf RIGHT NOW is a koan, a riddle, a parable for you to solve before you can go on from that place. This is RIGHT NOW your (WHO?) God-given, provided purpose. So RIGHT NOW, sit down in the middle of yourSelf and your place and CENTER.

Your identity cannot do the job. "I can't do it" is the truth about the capabilities of the identity. Jesus made it clear that the identity is to the Christ-center as a crippled man (homo) is to a whole man. He held out THEWAY to be whole again. In the process, the identity must be abandoned.

God, nature, life, destiny, fate, cosmic energy, random chance—whatever—gave each of us life: body, brains, and time. (God gave to WHO?) He gave us the brains to decide what to do with this body in the time allotted. If the body and brains are tools given to us by God, then WHO? received the gift? The Christ-center is the only answer. The identity is then merely a tool of the Christ-center. This reality is brought into realization (reality) by the process of centering, the actualizing (making actual) process of bringing the Christ-center into command of the organism: the space suit.

By definition, God is able to do the job and cure the crippled (limited) identity. Surrender that identity to the command of the center—to WHOM? God gave the gift.

"Surrender," "submission," "humbleness," "defenselessness" all stem from a firm base in OKness. A firm dependence on God absolutely requires no defenses (see aichito). Defenses are the tools of the identity—necessary when one is operating in AND OF this world. They are useless, ignorant, irrelevant, and counterproductive when operating in the world BUT OF the Christ-center: God.

CHAPTER XV

COSMIC REALITY: So science tells us that there is matter and there is energy, and each are transmutable into the other. We can see, perceive, grasp, and use forms and even manipulate energy as it passes us. But pure energy is, of itself, not a thing, immaterial (not material), but a flux, a flowing, a happening action itself: something occurring here and now in the present, neither a possibility nor a certain event. Thus, there is space (we suppose or assume), and it is filled with flowing energy doing all sorts of things (?).

We cannot see light; when photons impinge on our retinas, we see the source of the light, but we do not see the light itself. Sunlight illuminates our world, but we only see reflected light from some object that is being illuminated just so we can see it. But between our eyes and that object, a multitude of photons pass through; they do not impede our vision, for we cannot see them: we cannot see light. Light (photons) streams outward in a continuously expanding spherical continuum from every star. One star alone is sufficient to fill all space with light. But when one considers the trillions of light sources, one experiences the truth that space is filled to overflowing. Concentrate this night on a single star; its photons strike your retina and you see its ancient light. But there are also photons from that star falling on your cheeks, at your feet, over the entire earth, and passing through and outside the solar system. Space is crammed with energy. Our arrogance thinks we have experienced a star when only an infinitely tiny bit of light has impinged on our retinas. It is only our ignorance that sees space as empty. And our arrogance that swells the tiny retinal receptor surface into cosmic truths.

*

What is our relation to reality? We think that the things that appear to our consciousness are real: that this desk, table, hand, pen, wall, auto, and computer are solid reality. But we are mistaken.

Consider the rainbow as our metaphor. There are three necessary components to a rainbow: (1) a thin scattering of falling raindrops, (2) a brightly shining sun whose rays can reach those raindrops, (3) an observer situated at the proper angle of refraction/reflection of the sun from those raindrops. A rainbow is considered an ephemeral illusion for it depends upon the presence of a lattice-like work of raindrops to spread the color spectrum to the eye.

It is also considered a gift from God. When one considers that an infinitesimally small part of the photons from the sun's nuclear fires stream out of the heavens, crossing 93 million miles to strike one specific globe of water dancing to the tunes of gravity and wind and reflect back into this tiny eye so as to impact on a rod or cone in hir retina—this is one of nature's miracles.

But if there is no eye present at that specific location, there will be no rainbow seen. Is there then a rainbow? No, there are only reflected light rays passing through that location. There must be an observer at the precise location to experience those light rays as a rainbow.

Thus, two observers standing shoulder to shoulder both see and experience a rainbow. But is it the same rainbow? No. The angle of incidence is so precise that each experiences different light rays reflecting from different raindrops. Thus each observes a different illusion. A specific rainbow is a specific and independent experience for each observer.

What does this illusion have to do with reality? Science has disclosed to us that all matter is composed of a latticework of atoms and/or molecules. Most volume of an atom or molecule is empty space. What appears to our macro eye as solidity is empty space with a thin web of tiny bits of matter (the nucleus) circled by even smaller electrons cycling in that space. The matter of an atom is infinitesimal in contrast to the space involved. The solidness is experienced because of the forces that bind these atoms and molecules together. As we touch a surface our sense receptors feel those forces acting— we do not feel a surface.

Man sees when light rays (photons) impinge on the forces of the crystal lattice of atoms and molecules and are reflected back to the observer's retina. This is precisely the process to be found in the making of a rainbow. Without an observer, THERE IS NO DESK, PEN, HAND, AUTO, WALL, COMPUTER—or rainbow. There is just reflected light passing through space. For these things to exist, in addition to the crystal web, BOTH LIGHT and AN OBSERVER are necessary.

*

If energy has no form (and, by definition, it does not), then we cannot distinguish it from the void: the space in which it exists. That concept is the result of our materialistic linguistics. Thus, we can realize that the truth is that there can be but ONE "out there." The cosmos is, therefore, ONLY pure (uncontaminated), undefined (without form) energy. Thus, moves the unfathomable forces of God in existence. It is, by definition, eternal, for, being undefined, it is unlimited in its extent time-wise, also. It is omnipresent, omnipotent, and omniscient (insofar as knowledge exists at all, such must be contained within ALL that actually exists). These three words are used to define humanity's God. Thus, the reality of the cosmos and the truth concerning God must be equivalent.

It is from this vast, OMNIpresent, OMNIpotent, unlimited flow, source of energy, power, force that all forms arise. Our science tells us that (somehow) the energy is arranged in lattices of whirling condensed energy (called electrons) and an unlimited number of infinitesimally small points of matter. And these lattices form (are somehow arranged) into groupings that are further joined into various organizations. These forms (formations?) are only existent insofar as they are able to be perceived at all (by whom?). Thus, there is, of necessity, required the energy to create and maintain these forms (trees or mountains), the energy (sunlight) to illuminate them, and the energy to create, maintain, and empower the perceiver. And all these energies arise from the same cosmic reality-source.

God is not "out there" somewhere. That is a concept of arrogance in that it separates man (the perceiver) from the thing perceived (God or the cosmos: cosmic reality). That energy is here in us, with us, around us—WE ARE IT; we are in it, in the midst of it, and we live, move, and have our being because of it and in it (not "it," a thing, however, but the pure energy itself: live, moving, happening). A boulder, a stream, a moose, a bacterium, a human—each of these must cease to exist if the energy that supports it were to cease.

*

WHO? ARE WE: Thus, through all sorts of complicated twistings (DNA) and turnings (choices made through the millennia) and eons of evolution, humanity has come about, been created, happened. People are creations of the cosmic reality-source, whatever name we give to it (but not "thing," remember). The human is clearly distinguishable from the other animals by several points, among which are hir sizable brain, intellect, and language and hir opposable thumb, tool-making, and utilizing. This can all be reduced to the fact that this level in the hierarchical organization of the cosmic reality is the level that most effectively (anti-entropy behavior distinguishes life from nonlife) struggles against eternal entropy: man builds. S/he has such intentionality that s/he makes, creates, forms hirself—not merely out of programmed instinct, but as a result of hir own will.

But thereby, man is an anomaly, a sport, something different from the rest. In this confusion, our ideation bogs down; for, being unable to deal with reality, we have reverted back to conditioned abstractions, illusions, rationalizations, ideologies. If so, then just what are we? First, we must accept the truth that that vast, unlimited, eternal, omnipotent, omnipresent, omniscient reality has organized itself (some part of that energy) into ME: whoever is doing the thinking, writing, wondering, questioning, reading—YOU, sir, madam. It is not an abstraction or generalization (man); it is reality: the existence of the individual himself. What I am is, and ONLY is, can be nothing else—(1) an invisible matrix of cosmic energy (2) organized by that cosmic reality (3) into (a) that lattice and organization (b) which that energy flux determined (desired, wanted).

But am I thus the body? Man is sufficiently different from all the rest as to allow distinguishing ideation. So the scientists call us *Homo sapiens* as a class of primate, a vertebrate animal. As "homo," we are instinctually driven and thus correctly perceived as determined. We are conditioned, imprinted, and driven animals. But are we more than that? If so, we need another concept and another label for it. If we are "more," then it must be the difference aforementioned: that man has will. But we must carefully use the label "man" to refer to this something "more" that distinguishes hir from the other animals. By definition, "homo" is NOT distinguishable from the animals; s/he IS animal.

So now we have two concepts: one is the organized cosmic energy that we call "homo" and the other is "man," which is "homo + X." But there is no X, which can be OTHER than some part of that cosmic reality/energy. Thus, whatever the "+X" is, it IS another part of the cosmic energy flow. And we know that to be intentionality, or "WILL." Thus, it is, by definition and of necessity, that that intentionality or will can be and ONLY IS the intentionality of cosmic reality: the WILL of GOD.

The human animal, homo, is born weak and defenseless, like the tabula rasa (not quite, however) of literature. Upon that infant is inscribed not only the experiences that it has of its parents and its environment, but also the conclusions, decisions, and choices that it makes about those events and happenings. "Will" is personified in the sum of these choices and creates a persona or identity that all others will know and identify as this specific individual.

Let us now look at the finished product in the light of this knowledge of the reality of the cosmos. Our first rule is to speak only of "self" as individual and stay away from generalizing. There is intentionality at the center of this individual, and it lives in this organism, being, life, in this identity or form. Its original form has been modified by its environment but also, and more importantly, by its own choices and conclusions made as it grew and developed into its present self. The metaphor that I suggest for clarity is, "WE" (WHO?) are the raw energy of the cosmos specifically sent (projected) here on earth (this particular planet), and "we" are given the necessary tool to adapt and act hereon: our body—HOMO. We are individuals existing in a space suit designed to adapt us to the conditions of this planet. That space suit's design was originally at the WILL of its maker: the cosmic reality-source—pure energy (GOD). But as it grew, developed, learned, it modified itself to its specific environmental niche as best it was able and created a modified space suit with specific personality traits: the identity.

But we must be careful not to confuse our personal existence with the space suit that we wear: our body. Our being is pure cosmic energy individuated and supplied with the necessary means of operations on any planet, including this one. "WE," "US," "OUR," "I," "YOU," is not our body, our personality, or our identities (labeled with our names), but an individuated part of the vast, unlimited, omnipotent, omnipresent, omniscient cosmic energy, reality, source: GOD.

*

We are "ANGELS." But don't use that word trippingly; remember that you will unconsciously load that word with conditioned contamination. Use it correctly:

ANGEL = ANGELUS (Lat.) = ANGELOS (Grk.): messenger
akin to ANGAROS: mounted courier
both from an unknown Oriental source.
The early Christian writers (c. AD 300) consciously chose this word to translate the Hebrew "MAL'AKH": messenger—to carry this specific meaning.

ANGELOS = AN-GEL-AZ; ANGAROS = AN-GAR-AZ
AN-: other; beyond; -AZ: s/he who or that which
+ GEL > GAL: to call, shout; to be able, to have power
+ GAR: to call, cry; > GER: to cry hoarsely; to awaken
THUS, an ANGEL is s/he who is able, has the power,
to shout, cry, call beyond and awaken the other.
MESSENGER = MESSAGIER (Old Fr.) = MESSAGE

= MISSATICUM (Vulg. Lat.): something sent, a communication
= MITTERE (Lat.) (past part MISSUS = MISS + AZ):
    to send (that which is thrown) = SMEIT (PIE): to throw
THUS, a MESSENGER is one who has something,
    a communication, to project (throw).
COURIER = COURIER (Old Fr.)
    = CORRIERE (Old Ital.): a runner = CORRERE
    = CURRERE (Lat.): to run = KRS (X-P ?) = KERS (PIE): to run.

THUS, a COURIER is one who runs, and a MOUNTED COURIER is one who speeds up the process. A messenger has always been a runner, running to carry a communication speedily.

What does this mean to us? An angel is a mounted courier. And what is s/he mounted on (or in)? Answer: a space suit—the organism adapted to the environment into which s/he is sent. An angel existing in hir space suit comes to earth to bring a message (i.e., s/he is a messenger). Two questions become imperative: (1) what message does s/he bring, and (2) to whom does s/he bring it? Taking the second first: there is only one reality in existence—the cosmic reality. God speaks only to God, for there is no other alternative. But an angel IS individuated; thus, the messenger speaks to other individuated energies in their space suits. Never forget that the messenger does NOT speak to space suits; s/he speaks to MAN (individuated God), not homo, not the identity.

That leads to the conclusion that each of us are angels in our space suits on this earth and that within each of us, there is that individuation (spark) of the cosmic reality/energy/source. I (WHO?) am a messenger, as are you. Neither of us may realize this reality; neither of us may actualize it, and neither of us may want to accept it. We are in love and identify with our conditioned and determined self: identity. If so, we are in love with and identify with our tool: our space suit. The body exists only to give each of us the operational capacity of action on earth here to carry and deliver our message. So what is the message?

You don't believe that we are each and all angels?

BUDDHA = BU (BHEU) + DHE: to put, place, set (down)
　　　　THUS, put into action, motion, happening, being
　　　　THUS, make occur, happen, establish
　　　　THUS, establish the BU, make it happen.
BHEUDH: to be or to make aware (from Indo-European)
　　= BHEU (PIE): to be, exist, grow + DHE (PIE): set, put, etc.
THUS, BUDDHA = to put growth into existence or make growth happen;
AND as it grows, it becomes AWARE = awareness
BEO-DAN (Old Eng.): proclaim = BID
BUDON (Teut.) = BODA (Old Eng.): messenger
　　= BODIAN (Mid. Eng.): to announce: BODE
BUD-il-az = BYDEL (Old Eng.): herald = BEADLE (Lt. Eng.): messenger
BUDAN (Teut.) = BODH (Old Norse): command, omsBUDsman
THUS, the roots states that BUDDHA is he who grows in awareness is also a messenger.

A messenger exists to make others AWARE of hir message by proclaiming, announcing, communicating the commandment.

A messenger is also one who is AWARE that s/he has a message, and hir purpose to deliver it, commanded (set into motion = created for this purpose) by the sender of the message: an announcement for those to whom s/he carries it.

Using the feudal-king metaphor, a commoner is nonexistent until ratified, accepted, and acknowledged by the king, lord. A role for the commoner only comes into existence when the king/commander makes or creates the role and fills it with individuation. But that person only exists in order to fulfill the king's purpose, desire, wish, command, will.

THUS, it is our immediate need to become AWARE that each of us are individuated ONLY to make others AWARE of some message sent by the cosmic force (etc.) that created us. What is that message?—the WORD, the LOGOS!

*

GOD'S WILL: Men have, in their limited sight, defined God and God's will as something apart from themselves. Thus, we have asked (pleaded) for knowledge of God's will as a thing "out there," which we might learn of, know, and determine. But through science, we now know of the invalidity of the externalization process. Man needs no rationalization, no external statement of truth to justify hir actions or hir being. We now know that there is no absolute in existence. The only absolute is the indefinable cosmic energy/reality/source, which defies absolutism through its capacity to take any form. And, in addition, it changes AS we perceive it, so that it always remains different from our perception.

Then what is the purpose of human existence? WATCH IT! We must carefully control our definitions. "Man" is not "homo," remember. The purpose of the space suit (homo) is to give man operational capability on this planet earth. What is the purpose for which man (homo + center) was created, individuated, and sent here to earth? The angel is a messenger. It is God's will that each angel carry the message to all other angels.

*

LOGOS: So, again, what is the message? But, sir, you're still looking for an absolute. You are still interpreting "message" to mean some abstraction, some generalization, some clear single statement that exists "out there" as a truth that you (WHO?) might apprehend or grasp. Not true! The message is a flow of that pure undefined, undiluted cosmic energy—the LOGOS (see page xxx): the Word of God—into the world through the will of an angel. But while it might make for exciting fireworks and other diversions, in order to be made relevant and thus of value, the LOGOS requires modulation to every particular place and events. And this is the purpose of individuating the cosmic energy into individual units: angels. We are messengers bringing into every moment of our stay here on earth, the omnipotent power of God, and modulating it to the specific needs of the situation before us. Yes, it sounds like situation ethics, and the concept is very parallel. But that term applies to the will of homo, the identity and the conditioned and determined animal, and not to the will of MAN: that individuated spark of cosmic energy—the messenger ANGEL of God: the cosmic reality.

Thus, the WILL of God for each of US (WHO?) is to translate cosmic energy through our (WHOSE?) WILL (which is also that cosmic energy) and make it relevant to, active and effective in, the environment, place, situation, transaction, happenings in which we find ourselves. Is there some sort of guideline to follow as we (WHO?) translate that energy? No, any such thing would be a form created by homo: an absolute, a truth "out there," and not the energy as is. Jesus told us that we were to DO unto others "that which you want others to do unto you": we are to make our own decisions, translations (free will). God's will is then, by definition, our (WHO?) will. "WILL" (whoever's) is cosmic energy flowing, happening, acting, making, taking effect. And we, these angels, are the agents of that cosmic reality on this present planet Earth.

What then is God's will? It is whatever form each of us (WHO?) gives it in each moment of our time in this environment of earth. God's will is what we make of it, what we make it into.

Men (homo) have striven for millennia after improving themselves, whether through education, discipline, athletics, competition, studies, practice, etc. But they have been improving their space suits, not themselves. There is nothing wrong with building a better space suit (other than overemphasis); the improved model will perform better as it is needed. But Self—that is, the true self, the center, the angel—cannot be improved on. In fact, it is perfection itself. It is the Christ-center, perfect just as it exists. It is part of God: thus perfect. It is not acceptable to God, for it IS GOD. It is the space suit that is acceptable to God (the individuated angel) as we have made it, honed it, perfected it as we (WHO?— the angel) choose. We are OK by the nature of our being; we are not capable of ANY improvement. The body, organism, identity, space suit is limited, of course, by its adaptation to the exigencies of this environment. Our racial (innate, native, interstitial) belief that we (WHO?) are NOTOK arises from our confusion of Self with self: man with homo, and the Christ-center, ANGEL, with our body, ego, personality, identity, space suit.

(Note: The confusion must end. E. C. Whitmont's *Return of the Goddess* [Crossroad, 1982], page 110: "The repressed impulse lives on in a distorted unconscious fashion. It is projected upon our 'guilty' fellow man and woman." Note 3 : Disidentification rather than repression [i.e., distorted by later interpretation as a call for repression] is possibly also the implication of the sayings of Jesus. "If your right eye cause you to sin, pluck it out and throw it away... And if your right hand cause you to sin cut it off and throw it away" [Matthew 5:30–31]. But the Zen: "Kill yourself" leads to the truth— neither your eye nor your hand "caused" your sin. "YOU" (WHO?) did. Thus, if "you" caused the sin, cut IT off and discard IT!)

Thus, it is ourSELF that is the message! According to McLuhan, the medium (this organism, identity) is the message. We know that HOW we communicate a message is more important than the content of the message itself. Thus, we communicate by our behavior. WHAT passes across lies in the eye (or ear) of the beholder (perceiver). What you see is what you get! Each of us must make our own decisions about what we see in the world—what the meaning of another's behavior is. But we are always seeing only the message from God. But no matter how distorted the message seems, it is more relevant than we, in our arrogance, will admit.

Each of us angels brings the cosmic reality into the world and, with our free-willed choice of behaviorisms, directs it, whether we are awake or asleep, whether we are response-able or not. It is a MIRACLE!

MIRACLE = MIRACULUM (Lat.): that which is wondered at;
ALSO MIRAGE = MIRER (FR): to look at = MIRARE
ALSO MIRROR = MIROIR (Old Fr.) = MIRARE
from MIRARE: to wonder at = MIRUS: wonderful
    = SMEI (PIE): to laugh, smile = SMIRK, SMILE
    = SMEI-RO: causing one to smile
    = (s) MIR-AZ = MIROS (Lat.): wonderful
THUS, MIRACLE is that abnormal, unusual, unexpected external event or happening to which one responds with such pleasure that it brings a smile to the face: the "aha!" phenomena.

CHAPTER XVI

Is there any duty to communicate any of these truths? The Christian ideology is that you must be a witness. All right, but consider semantics once again. What does "witness" mean? It does NOT mean that you are to TELL, preach at, others. It means that you have witnessed (seen: perceived) the truth—that you have been AWAKE and WATCHed, and that you saw, like a witness to a crime or accident has perceived what has happened. Catch hold of those words: "WATCH" and "SEE"; they are biblical. WHO? is the witness? Obviously, by definition, it is the observer who is the witness. WHO? then is the observer? WHO? received the gift. (That's not a question, that's a statement.)

WITNESS = WITNESSE (Mid. Eng.): to testify; one who has knowledge
    = WITNES (Old Eng.) from WIT: knowledge
WIT (Teut.): knowledge, intelligence, wise man: one who knows
the ability to know AND the coordinate ability to express
from WID (PIE): to see
    = WITAN: to look after or guard, show the way = gUIDe (Fr.)
    = WIDTO = WISSAZ: the known
THUS, the certain or sure = GEWISS (Ger.)
    = WIDE = VIDE (Lat.), VIDERE: to see
    = VEOIR = VEUE = VEWE = VIEW
    = VISUS: sight = VISION; VISUALIZE
+ E = EX: completely + seen = EVIDENT; EVIDENCE = the data:
      (the completely seen, thus known) that supports a judgment.
    = WIDESYA = IDEYA (Grk.) = IDEA: appearance, form, idea
    = WIDTOR = WHIDZTOR = HIDSTOR = HISTOR (Grk.): wise, learned
    = WOIDO = VOIDA (Aryan) = VEDA (Sanskrit):

I have seen = I know = knowledge

AND WEID (PIE): to see
    = WEID-TO = WISSAZ (Teut.) = WIS-AZ: s/he who or that which
    = WISE: that which or s/he who sees: s/he sees, the Seer
    = WISDOM the realm of seeing: knowing THUS learned.
    = WISSON: appearance, form, manner: WISE, gUISe
    = also WEID + AZ = WEIDOS = form, shape = EIDOS (Grk.)
    = A: not + EIDOS (VISible or form) = Ah-EID-AZ
THUS, inVISible or without form = HA-AIDES = HADES
THUS, a WITNESS not only has sight, but has SEEN IT, THUS knows
and recognizes its form and appearance (such a one has intelligence),
and THUS has certain knowledge of the thing seen and inferentially is
able to communicate that knowledge—its history or story.

First, you must gain your own center—center yourself. Then, you
will be able to pass the word, the LOGOS. But "logos" is not ideological
rhetoric or doctrinal garbage. What is the "LOGOS"? That is a question
of semantics, not beliefs. The "logos" is the Word of God, the power
issuing from the Christ-center and not anything OF the identity.

LOGOS from LOGOS (Grk.) = LOGAZ from LEG (PIE): collect, gather
    + AZ: s/he who or that which: gatherer or collec-tor/-tion
    = LOGOS (Grk.): speech, word, reason as in LOGic,
        apoLOGy, proLOGUE, LOGarithm, sylLOGism, anaLOGous
    = LEGEIN (Grk.): gather, speak = LEXicon, diaLECT, cataLOGUE
    = LEKJAZ (Teut.) = speaker of magic words = enchanter
    = LAECE (Old Eng.): physician = LEECH
    = LEGERE (Lat.): gather, choose, pluck, read = LECture, LEGend
        LEGible, colLECT, eLECT, LESSON, intelLIGent, sacriLEGE
    = LEG-NO: that which is gathered = LIGNUM (Lat.): firewood
    = LEG: collection of (rules) = LEX (Lat.):
        law, LEGAL, LEGitimate, LEGislate, LOYal, priviLEGE
    = LEGARE (Lat.): to engage by contract = to deputize,
        commission, charge = LEGacy, alLEGE, colLEAGUE, deLEGate
THUS, LEG, LOG = the gathering of ideas, concepts, symbols, words
that is recognized by the speech of the adept; and the resultant
collection of same such as in books, a group of laws or a contract,

or in a mind or abstract mind: reason. The meaning of LOGOS, as in the Word of God, is the collecting together in one place, obviously the human mind, of a collection as above defined, which motivates a communication perceived by someone as so far beyond ordinary speech and thinking as to be classified as divine.

In our daily lives, in this culture, in this age, with this created identity, we make many communications, conversations, statements, for we live in a verbal, intellectual, scientific milieu, or medium. Here words are essential to the continuance and maintenance of the existing structure of things: the status quo (the common consensus of donJuan).

If we wish to change things (as we do from moment to moment with our wives, our children, our homes, our auto mechanics, our taxes, our crowds, our pollution, and our own insecurities), we use the common tool—we communicate (if only to ourselves). But we ERR as long as the identity commands the organism, and we are speaking homo to homo. We are then speaking to the other's center of RESISTANCE, where hir defenses are, where s/he is prepared for fight or flight. Talking to homo's intellect awards hir the power to pick and choose what s/he desires from your words. Besides, "swine" cannot use "pearls" for nourishment, only for exploitation.

Remember, speaking to another's identity, intellect, ego requires the use of power to overcome hir defenses and resistances. We will never gain a friend, a convert, through overpowering hir. And persuasion is power. S/he will always resent the conquest. "A man convinced against his will, is of the same opinion still."

Consider this absurdity: if we were to meet Jesus, the Christ, on our road (way) of life to anywhere, would we stop to TELL him how awful life is, like, "Did you know that the school system is producing millions of young people totally unprepared to meet the demands of the socio/econo/politico/cultural environment? Why don't you doooooo something about it?" If Christ be God and if God creates only what s/he wants, then (*a*) s/he already knows about the problem, and (*b*) s/he wants it that way! It is absurd to think that YOU (WHO?) are THEONE who knows what God is IGNORANT of and that it is YOU who MUST (compulsion) TELL HIR all about it. Who did you really think you were talking to? WHO?

*

THE CENTERING AFFIRMATION

I SEE, I KNOW, I ACKNOWLEDGE, IT IS A FACT THAT
in my life, RIGHT NOW,
GOD, the Father within,
is actually actively activating and actualizing
everything that I need—THANKS!

In the process of prayer, the supplicant retains the power to frame what it is s/he wants and, by doing so, deprives hir "Lord" of choice. By this process, s/he (hir ego/identity) maintains hirself as the real God. Thus, it is error to pray for some specific when God knows what is best. In fact, in God's mind, there probably is something better than what I am asking for. It is I who am blind to that better that is, in fact, now available to me, if only I were open-minded enough to see it. So I ought to pray for sufficient open-mindedness and open-eyedness so that I may see and apprehend the good NOW already there for me, instead of being compulsively focused on the negative/problem.

Thus, God has available now for me all the good, abundant supplies that I can ever have a need, use, or want for. I refuse to see that truth by being addicted and obsessed with being asleep and afraid to be awake. Awareness, awakeness is the cure.

THUS, I PRAY for the awakeness, awareness, open-eyedness, and open-mindedness to see and grasp the good, abundant supply that is already there for me.

The error in prayer is that one is asking for something to be done in the future. It is a focus on the obscure future rather than the concrete present. Inherent in the act of prayer is the belief, stance, or set that what is being asked for does not NOW exist: the denial of the "here and now." One of the names of God is "that which is." It is a shift of one's energy from reality (Jesus) to abstractions (the Christ). YHSWH being "here and now," that shift is the denial of Jesus.

Thus, it is that there can be no affirmation here. Any ideation is made by the ego/identity. The statement desired here is that of the center and that is being and action, not reflection. The center grasps its good; it does not pray, worry, think, or analyze.

Thus, I must cease praying, cease analyzing, cease thinking—and center. Prayer, thus, becomes a simple affirmation:

*

The cosmic energy, force, source
speaking through my Christ-center
and referring to this organism and
its ego, personality and identity, says:

"THIS IS MY BELOVED SON."

And, BEING ME,
has me exactly where I belong,
where HE is realizing and actualizing me,
HIS specific expression
and where I am receiving all that I need.

No, if you meet the Christ (I didn't say Jesus) on the road, I'm sure you really want to talk to hir, so DO SO. But since there is NOTHING (no-thing) to TELL hir, you can only PRAISE, LOVE, and THANK hir. Obviously, if you started: "Oooooh, I loooove you, Geezuz—praaaize the Lord, I thank you for all you've done for me," etc., ad nauseam, you would bore and embarrass him and divert hir from HIRWAY. That way is ideological bull shouted AT the man right in front of you and ignores the truth, which he promulgated: you are to praise, love, and thank GOD. In our present example, that does NOT mean JESUS; it means the Christ-center WITHIN him. WATCH IT!

WATCH that MAN! Yes, you're correct; that must be extended to every man whom we meet on our road (to Emmaus) of life.

But Christ speaks in the Spirit (logos). So you too must speak in the Spirit—with the tongues of angels. How is this done, then? First, BE CENTERED: the identity set aside. Then the center of the organism will be in command, and if that center WILLS something be done, it WILL be DONE. The center of this organism speaks to the center IN the other. The communication is the communication of God's energy (the logos), which is God's Will (what else?), and creates in that other the psychic set of OKness: being acceptable to God. Thus, you will speak from your own spiritual apparatus through the collective unconscious directly to the inner consciousness (un-, sub-, or super-) of the other—not in words, but in feelings, emotions—which control. And then no person is our enemy.

Can the identity DO THAT? Now, you're on the right track. Only God, the divine Christ-center has that capacity.

Consider: the example of meeting Christ on the road is NOT hypothetical. You are NOW and HAVE BEEN on the road—the WAY—all the time. In every person you meet, there is the Christ-center, whether actualized or not, whether s/he is aware of it or not. EVERY person has, at hir center, the Christ, although covered by the bushel basket of hir identity thus hidden, latent. God peeps shyly out of those eyes while command lies with the identity. If your Christ-center is in command of your organism, then you WILL speak (LOGOS) the word from your center to hir center, of which you are aware even though s/he is not. And what do you (WHO?) communicate? PRAISE, LOVE, and THANK the center—from center to center. As Brother Blue said, "I'm looking at you from the middle of the middle of me at the middle of the middle of you."

Is this done in verbal words? No, of course not. It is done in the LOGOS (weren't you told that earlier?). The flow of God's energy at God's WILL (not the identity's) in the form that God chooses. It is HIR choice of words, if any. This is the HIGHEST form of communication that can be—BY DEFINITION, again. When God (the Christ-center) speaks to God (another Christ-center), then it is God who defines all the communication: the motivations of all parties. All WANTS are satisfied by love, acceptance, reassurance, the end of alienation, and brotherhood, because what is truly needed is supplied. All things are possible with God (Christ-center). The only problems we have are ourselves, and there is only ONEWAY to solve them: self-help, Self-awareness.

*

PRAISE, LOVE, THANK

PRAISE = PREISEN (Mid. Eng.) = PRESIER (Old Fr.): to prize
    = PRETIARE (Late Lat.): to price
    = PRETIUM (Lat.): price, value, reward
    = PRETIO: worth, value, price -
      that opposite or equivalent (on the scales)
    = PRE-TI, PER (PIE): forward, through > first, chief >
      > near, in front of, opposite, against
PRIZE: to value highly, esteem. cherish, treasure
APPRAISE: to evaluate, to set a value on
APPRECIATE: to be fully aware of and sensitive to
the quality, value, significance, magnitude
THUS, PRAISE is to be fully aware of and sensitive to (and thus admire, esteem, treasure, and cherish) the quality, merit, worth, value (importance), significance (meaning and consequences), and magnitude of something. For one to be certain that the other is so aware, etc., they must speak of it.

THANK: to hold responsible, blame, credit (appraise),
express gratitude
    = THANCIAN (Old Eng.) = THANKON (Teut.) = TONG (PIE): to
      feel
TONG = THANKON (Teut.) = THENKAN (Old Eng.): to THINK
    = THAUGHT (Teut.) = THOT (Old Eng.): THOUGHT
    = THUNKJAN (Teut.)
    = THYNCAN (Old Eng.): to appear or seem
THUS, THANK (THINK) is to hold responsible, blame, credit someone for the quality, merit, worth, value, significance, consequences of something. Again for one to be certain that the other does hold correctly, they must speak of it.

LOVE: concern, fondness, enthusiasm, devotion, adoration for something to the point of giving goods, kindness, and mercy
    = LUFU (Old Eng.) = LUBO (Teut.) = LUBHA (PIE)
    = LEUBH: to care, desire, love
    = LEUBHO = LIUBAZ (Teut.): beloved = LIEF
    = LOUBH = LAUBO (Teut.)

= LEAF (Old Eng.): permission: pleasure, approval = LEAVE
= LAUBO = geLAUBO
= GELEAFA, BILEAFA (Old Eng.) = BELIEF: faith
= GALAUBJAN: to hold dear, pleasant, esteem, trust
= GELEFAN, BELEFAN (Old Eng.): BELIEVE, trust
= LEUBH = LUBHE = LIBERE (Lat.): to be dear, pleasing
= LIBIDO (Lat.): pleasure, desire

THUS, LOVE is based on the pleasure principle: we love that which pleasures us and which gives us pleasure. We desire, cherish, hold dear, esteem, care about, and love what we find pleasure in. And that which repeatedly gives us more and more pleasure (doesn't wear out or wane) we trust, approve of, and finally, have faith in and believe.

AMOUR (Fr) = AMOR (Lat.) = AMARE: to love
= AMMA (Lat.): mother, AMAH
= MA (PIE): mother = an imitative root derived from the child's cry for the breast (a linguistic universal found in many of the world's languages—often reduplicated) = MAMMA, MAMMALIA
= MAIA (Grk.) good mother or nurse
= MAYA (Sanskrit): the great goddess, mother
of the universe and all the "ten thousand things"

ALSO AMICUS (Lat.): friend
Friendship then is based on some kind of nurture.
THUS, AMOUR emphasizes the nurturingness of motherlove. Motherlove is distinguished from fatherlove in that motherlove accepts the child unconditionally; she loves merely because s/he is—is in BEing.
THUS, LOVE and AMOUR do NOT translate. LOVE is based on the pleasure principle—we love so long as we are pleased while AMOUR is unconditionally based on mere existence: BEing.
BRINGING the conclusions from above TOGETHER here:

PRAISE is to be fully aware of and sensitive to (and thus admire, esteem, treasure, and cherish) the quality, merit, worth, value (importance), significance (meaning and consequences), and magnitude of something.

THANK (THINK) is to hold responsible, blame, credit (assign, ascribe, attribute to) someone for the quality, merit, worth, value, significance, consequences of something. (Who is that someone? It is THAT whose qualities we are speaking of.)

LOVE is based on the pleasure principle; we love that which pleasures us and which gives us pleasure. We desire, cherish, hold dear, esteem, care about, and love what we find pleasure in. And that which repeatedly gives us more and more pleasure (doesn't wear out or wane) we trust, approve of, and finally, have faith in and believe. We love something so long as we are pleased by it.

AMOUR emphasizes the nurturingness of motherlove.
Motherlove is distinguished from fatherlove in that motherlove accepts the child unconditionally; she loves merely because s/he is— in being.
For one to be certain that an "other" does praise, thank, and love correctly, they must speak about it.

CONCLUSION

To PRAISE, one must be fully aware of and sensitive to and
admire, esteem, treasure, and cherish X ;
to THANK, one must hold responsible,
blame or credit someone for, and
assign, ascribe, attribute X to someone;
to LOVE, one must desire, cherish, hold dear, esteem,
and care about X;
and AMOUR, one must unconditionally accept and nurture X;

X being the quality, merit, worth, value, importance, magnitude of, and the significance, meaning, and consequences of THAT which pleasures us. Remembering that THAT which repeatedly gives us more and more pleasure (doesn't wear out or wane) we trust, approve of, and finally, have faith in and believe. Repetitive reinforcements ultimately condition us into a set.

("Do unto others AS YOU WOULD HAVE THEM DO UNTO YOU"
    = that which you desire, like that which pleases you.)
For one to be certain that an "other" does praise, thank, and love correctly, they must speak about THAT.

What practically is it that we should praise, thank, and love? Since at the center of any—and all—sits the Christ, six-point, everyone qualifies. There is no individual to find; there is only the Christ to see. So we join everyone in our sitting, study, meditation, prayer, and action. That they are less advanced is irrelevant, for we are speaking to their center; we commune only with the Christ, we meet them at the six-point of transfiguration, we do not speak to or at their intellect, and we harmonize with their Shushumna. We do nothing for them, for God has no need for our services. We only praise, love, and thank God, Christ, the other for HIR and OUR BEING—BHE-ing.

Praise, love, and thank projected at an "other" amounts to one central idea: that he is entitled to the same praise, love, and thanks that each of us owes to God. That lets our esteem for God be projected on the other person and makes him feel as esteemed as God. The building of Self-esteem for Self is THEWAY for all people in all times and in all places.

This is the way of Jesus, Buddha, of the Sufi, Tao, Zen:

> Renouncement of the ways and values OF the world (wer-aldh);
> Death to the ego; rebirth of the new man;
> Absolute trust in Allah, God, nature, truth;
> Our own virtue, morality, righteousness, enlightenment, and salvation leads to the same for the "other";
> Sitting, study, meditation, prayer, action, behavior—

Focus is on bringing into actualization, realization, being:
YHWH/YHSWH/YAM/SUCHNESS/CENTER/CHRIST
(the (6) six point of transfiguration)

PRACTICE: one must
    be fully aware of and sensitive to X;
    hold responsible, blame, credit someone (6) for X;
    assign, ascribe, attribute to someone (6) X;
    admire, cherish, esteem, care about, and desire X.

X is the quality, worth, importance, significance, meaning, and consequences of THAT which pleasures us; remembering that THAT which gives us enduring pleasure, we trust, approve of, have faith in, and believe—and speak about, proclaim all of it.

Ultimately, it is our God-given existence/life/BEing that allows us even the idea of pleasure. And when we accept that unconditionally, life becomes abundance and pleasure becomes bliss.

And THAT BEing is YHWH: YHSWH =
    YAM THAT WHICH, HERE AND NOW, YAM!

CHAPTER XVII

What is the duty for THIS angel? "This" = ME, YOU!
"OBEY GOD" has been the word (LOGOS) for over two thousand years.

OBEY, OBEDIENCE = OBOEDIENS (Lat.), OBOEDIRE: listen to, hear
    = OB: (intensive), to, toward, in front of, on account of
    + AUDIRE: to hear, attend to (see page xxx)
    = AW, AU: to hear + DHE: to put, place or set
    = AUDHE (Grk.): to feel; AUDIRE (Lat.): to hear
    = the power to place one's perception or attention.
THUS, OBAWDHE, OBAUDHE, OBeD (where *e* is the neutral sound
OBAHD, OBEHD): to intensively place one's perception or attention
steadfastly at, toward, on, or over something and feel and perceive it
with the same intensity.

(PERCEPTION from PERCIPERE: to seize wholly
from PER: thoroughly + CAPERE: to seize
    from CAP = KAP (PIE): to grasp or handle;
        also = (K) HABEN: to have and/or to hold.
THUS, to take hold of something thoroughly, absolutely.)

THUS, OBEY = to have such an intense conscious control of one's
organs of reception that s/he is able to take a thorough conceptual
hold on something—rather than one's prior conceptions, thus to hear
what is truly going on.

    This capacity is to hear not only the surface message but
also the hidden message. Coming from families in which every
message is contaminated, one concludes that (1) every message is

always contaminated; (2) that all contaminations arise out of fear, hate, anxiety, anger, hostility; (3) NEVER from love, admiration, acceptance, joy; and therefore (4) are bad, evil, negative, upsetting, not helpful, carry no vital or necessary information; and (5) thus must be screened out absolutely. No one can handle inconsistent messages: you either screen out the contamination or the verbality thrown at you. That way leads to confrontation and pain for an infant.

From this arises the conditioned response: ignore, screen out, or discount all the contaminations in any messages. Thus, one listens only superficially (to the face value). One HEARs intently and deeply all the surficial details of what is said, but NOTHING further; anything further would be useless and irrelevant. Thus, much is lost. If one listens more deeply, s/he would find information about the person speaking. Not good nor bad, just information. Not looking deeply, the center of that person cannot be seen.

OBEDIENCE is not, as is popularly defined, the requirement to follow orders as in the military. It is that which is involved in the admonition "to listen." One may hear (AUDIO), but not HEAR. S/he places hir attention on hir opponent, but s/he fails to perceive hir as friend at hir center. S/he is not listening to the depths of hir communication: from hir center. S/he has failed to direct hir perception toward hir. Hir ears (sensory receptors), yes, but not hir perception. S/he is rebellious in that s/he refuses to be obedient; obedience being the opposite of rebellion.

There is no necessity to OBEY because one MUST; there is no force involved at all. S/he is OBEDIENT when s/he CHOOSES FREELY to perceive the reality in the other. God made humanity free: that is, FREE WILL—obedience is a freely made choice at the will of the individual.

The difference between the devil and God is that the devil DEMANDS that obedience be equated with individuality. Being submissive, supplicant, and obedient is to sell your soul. To take a job in a bureaucracy REQUIRES loyalty to their values. The devil attempts to overpower one's independence, individuality, and FREE WILL by subtle manipulations.

DEVIL = DEOFEL (Old Eng.), DEBEL (as in "de Debel made me do it")
 = DIABOLUS (Lat.) = DIABOLOS (Grk.): the slanderer

= DIABALLEIN: to slander, set at variance
= DIA: across + BALLEIN: to throw = throw across
= GWEL (PIE): to throw, reach; dance; beam, ray
   also BOULE (Grk.): a throwing forward of the mind
    > determination, will
= EMBLEM: to throw out
= HYPERBOLA: to throw beyond > exceed> exaggeration
= METABOLISM: to throw into something else > change
= PARABLE = PARABOLARE (Lat. <Grk.): to throw beside
   > to compare > a comparison
= PARLIAMENT; PARLEY = PARABOLARE: discourse, talk
   > place for talking
= PAROLE (Fr. <Lat. <Grk.): a word spoken > oath, promise
= PROBLEM (Grk.): thing thrown forward
   > a question or situation proposed for consideration
= SYMBOL = SUMBOLON (Grk.): thrown together
   > token for identification

THUS these indicate he who opposes with words and thus
slanders, accuses, disagrees, sets at variance
is the accuser, adversary:
one who throws objections, differences,
including facts and truth, in one's way.
SATAN = SATAN (Heb.): devil, adversary = SATAN: to accuse

It becomes clear then that the preachers of this world who go out of their way to exploit people's native doubt by throwing convincing arguments in their faces are DEVILS, by definition.

*

God, on the other hand, merely ASKS obedience with no question of one's individuation or identity or even loyalty. Your identity (no matter how strange, different, absurd, or abnormal) is OK as is and acceptable (there is no alienation). God merely recommends that you choose to place your perception toward (outward) the reality, which comprises your present environment and away from your infantile subconsciously controlled conditioning. But God doesn't DEMAND

ANYTHING, not even that one SHOULD join hir team or army. S/he does not supply uniforms or a creed or a list of any specific behaviors, just OBEDIENCE by your (WHO?) personal choice.

We already belong to God's team because we were born that way: OK, IN. Alienation is of our own creation. It happens as we pursue our individuation that we believe the surface of what we experience. We are on God's team unless and until we choose otherwise. In our infantile belief that we are alone, we alienate ourSelves from God's team. The WAY we PERCEIVE the world (REALITY) is dictated by our own CHOICES made while forming our identity. "GROWTH" means to look constantly deeper and deeper into our present experience and see the hand of God in it. We can only do this by placing, doing, setting our perception toward it: being OBEDIENT and observant (see page xxx).

We are to OBEY GOD, and wives are told to OBEY their husbands. Now we know that adhering to patriarchal commands is not what is meant by these admonitions. We are to control our own responses (response-ability), direct our sense receptors, look beneath the surface of what is there, listen deeply, and hear the central core (hidden) message: to perceive God in the midst of the world (wer-aldh, page xxx), and for wives to see and understand the depths of their husband's conditioning, needs, illusions: the WAY the Christ-center demonstrates itself in him.

You have been told to listen to others. So now, LISTEN so deeply (obey) that you can hear (perceive) the message (logos), which emanates from the others' Christ-center. And be flexible—your identity is not in command; therefore, you need no program (cook book); you have no hidden agenda (beliefs). You are only loving, or praising, and thanking. Put into words (or actions: behavior) your own set of OKness with the unlimited power of the Christ-center. The organism is no longer crippled by the dominance of the identity. It is God WHO? rules.

What is the meaning of "righteousness"? How the church sees it and the popular definition is not the question. The word is, of course, composed of "right-eous-ness." The meaning becomes clear (?) but full of redundancies. Both "-eous" and "-ness" are equivalents meaning: abounding in, having or possessing the quality or state of "right." Then, what is "right"? The root (see REG, page xxx) is to guide or rule (straight) or to be straight—upright. There is an inherent problem in the definitions:

RIGHT means
   conforming to justice (WHOSE?);
   undeviating from the true and just (WHO? determines truth);
   the straight course, obedience to authority, freedom from
   guilt and sin (WHOSE? authority determines these things);
   to do justice to, relieve others from wrongs
                    (according to WHOSE? judgment);
   a power or privilege to which one is entitled to upon principles of
                    morality, religion (WHOSE? principles).
   Obviously the word "right" sends us to the authority within, where there can be no external definitions for virtuous, worthy, godly, holy, or equitable.
   What then is it to be "righteous"? The world has always been in the greatest need for men a (and women) of "right." It is a sort of "situation ethics." That is, in order for one to be "right," one MUST take one's response-ability impeccably.

IMPECCABLE: flawless, without sin or wrongdoing
   = IMPECCABILIS (Lat.): not able to sin
   = IN: not + PECCARE (Lat.): to sin
   = PED (PIE): foot, leg > snare, fetters, trap
      > stumble, fall, worst > sin.
THUS, IMPECCABLE is to be so (response) able as not to stumble, err, fall, be trapped, or sin. Such demands an unwavering attention (see page xxx), the exclusion of secondary interests, without faltering, stumbling, or distraction, without wobbling (Tai Chi Chuan).

ULC doctrine is, one must do that which is right. Read: one MUST do THAT which is RIGHT (and one decides "that" for himself). This applies to every behaviorism.
   Every moment of our lives, we are beset with stimuli that prompt, DEMAND, and respond. S/he who makes righteous responses must be hewing to the "straight and narrow" path(WAY), thus not deviating from the true and just: living and doing "right." Through the existence of hir life, through the organism as hir tool, man will be

correct (righteous) and relieve others from wrong, do justice to the many. S/he that lives this WAY (THEWAY) is the counterweight to those of the left and the right, who push the masses left and right: the identity doing the will of the devil. The one commanded by the Christ-center will find that s/he (WHO?) has the POWER to which S/HE is entitled upon the principle of truth. S/HE is the ONE to whom we must look for salvation; s/he is the messenger who brings the LIGHT (HIR own) into the world.

*

MORAL = MORALS (Lat.) from MOS, MOR-: custom = ME- (PIE):
    = ME, myself, MY; MEI-no = MINE
    = in the middle of = ME-DHI (Teut.)
    = MID (Old Eng.): among, with
    = ME-TA = META (Grk.): between, with, beside, after
    = a quality of mind = MO-TO = MOTH-AZ (Teut.): mind, disposition, MOOD
    = MOS (Lat.): wont, humor, manner, custom
    = MORES, MORAL
    = to measure = ME-LO = MAELAZ (Teut.): MEAL, measure, mark (pieceMEAL) or appointed time for eating
    = ME-DH-IRE = METIRI (Lat.) (pp. MENS)
    = MENSURA: to measure = diMENsion, imMENSE
    = METRON (Grk.): measure, rule, length, proportion, METER
    = MEN, MENS, MENEN, MENOT: measure of time = MONTH, MOON
    = MAENON (Teut.) = MONA (Old Eng.): moon (MONday)
    = MENE (Grk.) = MENOpause, MENarche, MENiscus
    = MENSIS (Lat.) = MENSES, MENSTRUAL, seMESTER
    = MEDERI (Lat.): to heal = MEDICINE; MEDITARE = MEDITATE
    = MED (PIE): take appropriate measures, measure, fit
    = MODEST, MODE, MUST
    = ME (PIE): in the middle of + DHE (PIE):
    to set, put, place >establish, lay down, make happen
THUS, ME-DHE: to establish, lay down, make happen
something (rules, dogmas, measures) in the midst of
anything: self, others, the world > to lay down

and/or make appropriate measures, measuring happen.

THUS, ME = (a) me, myself, and mine lies in the middle of,
among, with me;
>   (b) the internal mind, disposition, mood leads to the set of wont,
>   humor that dictates the behavioral manner, custom, mores of
>   one, family, tribe, clan;
>   (c) the act of measuring—from the point to measure to/from mark
>   or appointed place and/or time yields the measure, rule, length,
>   proportion of space/time.

THUS, MORALITY is that entity that lies in the MIDST of MYSelf
and creates the inner MOOD, which METES out the psychic set that
dictates MY behavior, manner, Way that is MEASURED BY and that
MEASURES the social customs and MORES of my environment. That
psychic set and behavior that (both in time and place) is appropriate,
well-measured, and well-proportioned is MORAL—is the meaning
of MORAL. But not the common consensus from the midst of the
culture.

*

MEDIA (pl.) = MEDIUM (sing.) (Lat.): middle = MEDIUS: middle
>   = MEDHYO (PIE): MIDDLE = MEDIAL, MEDIAN, MEDIATE,
>   MEDIOCRE,
>   AMIDST, MEAN, interMEDIATE, MESO-(Grk.)
>   MED-DHYO = DHEY (PIE) (dhia): to see, look
>   = DHYA = DHY-MN = SEMA (Grk.):
>   thing seen (in the middle of data) > sign
>   = DHYATI (Sanskrit): s/he observes mentally
>   > s/he meditates (in the middle of self)

THUS, we turn the verb into a noun—from BEING IN the middle to
THE middle—from a verb into a gerund. Thus, MIDDLE, MEDIUM are
gerunds stating "it" is being in the midst.

MEDIUM: (i) occupying a position midway between extremes; being
between two degrees, amounts, quantities, polarities;

(ii) an intervening substance, agency, artistic materials through which something is accomplished, conveyed, transferred, transmitted, or expressed;

(iii) a surrounding environment in which something functions, thrives, grows, or happens;

THUS, the narrow extremes (polarities) are easily seen, grasped by the ordinary human mind while that in the great gray area of the middle is not experienced, felt, but IN which we live, move, and have our being. Politically, the extremes can be articulated and advocated, and constituencies marshaled about while it is the MEDIUM that is truly vital to life or success.

But while we are IN the MEDIUM by nature, we are not required to be OF it. It is discipline backed by understanding that FREES us. That God given power of free will allows us (WHO?) to adhere to THEWAY that passes straight down the MIDDLE without being obsessed, addicted, and compulsed into loyalty to any part or extreme OF it.

*

PHENOMENON/NEUMENON

PHENOMENON = PHENO-MEN-ON: an observable
(perceptible to the senses) event, fact
    = PHAENOMENUN (Lat.) = PHAINOMENON (Grk.)
    = PHAINOMENOS = PHAINO-MEN-OS:
      pres. part of PHAINESTHAI: to appear
    = PHAINEIN: to show = BHA (PIE)
BHA: to shine = (Teut.) BEACON, BECKON, BUOY, BERRY, BANNER
    = BHAWOS = BHAW-AZ = PHOS (Grk.): light = PHOSPHORUS,
      PHOTO-
    = BHANYO = PHAINEIN (Grk.): to bring to light
      > to cause to appear, show
    = PHAINESTHAI (pass): to be brought to light, appear
    = FANTASY, PHANTOM, PHASE, PHENOMENON,
      EMPHASIS, HEIROPHANT
THUS PHAIN@: to show, appear, make apparent (demonstrate)

or that which has been shown, demonstrated.

BHA: to speak = FARI (Lat.) = AFFABLE, FATE, INFANT, PREFACE
    = PHANI (Grk.): PROPHET, -FASIA
    = BANWAN (Teut.) = BANNS
    = BANNISH, BANDITS, BOON (prayer)
    = BHAMA = FAMA (Lat.): talk > reputation, fame
    = PHEME (Grk.): saying, speech = PHONE
    = BHATO = FATERI (Lat.): acknowledge, admit
    = CONFESS, PROFESS
THUS, PHAN@: to speak > make a saying (about something)
    > admit something.
THUS, BHA (PIE) as a root: the actor shows, demonstrates, thus making apparent something by action or speech.
THUS, PHENO something has been shown, become apparent, is now remark-able by a witness who observes, perceives, SEES.

NOUMENON (Ger.) (NOU-MEN-ON = NOUS-MEN-OS): object of intuition,
not accessible to the senses > the thing-in-itself
    = (Grk.): concept, thought = NOUEIN: to think, apprehend
    = NOUS (Grk.): reason, sense > mind, intellect
      > divine "understanding" = NOEsis, paraNOIA
    = GNO (PIE): KNOW, make KNOWN, declare, well-KNOWN, familiar,
ACQUAINT, KIN, get to KNOW, NOTE, CONNOTE, NOTICE, NOTIFY, COGNIZE, IGNORE, famous, NOBLE, GNOSIS, GNOMEN:
      one who points > judge: an expert NARRATES what he knows
      (NAME: see page xxx)

THUS, GNO@ (noo, new, nou) is rooted in the known, which is noted by the knower and communicated, first by pointing and then by declaration.
THUS, NOUS is the capability of understanding what is seen, noticed. We all SEE PHENOMENON, but the GNOSTIC SEER NOTICES the inner meaning, the not-so-obvious NOUMENON and points it out to us by some means of communication (speech): (BHA & SUPRA).

NEUMA (Lat.) = PNEUMA (Grk.): breath
    = PNEU (PIE): to breathe = SNEEZE (Teut.)
    = PNEU-MEN = PNEUMA (Grk.): breath, wind, spirit

NUMINOUS: the presence of the spirit (NUMEN)
    = NUMEN (Lat.): the "nod" of command > divine power, deity
      > the spirit in something
    = NEU (PIE): to shout
    = NUNTIUS (Lat.): ANNOUNCE > message > messenger
    : to nod = NUERI (Lat.): to nod (agreement), INNUENDO
    = NEU-MEN (Lat.): to nod > command > power > deity = NUMEN

NUMEN = PNEUM-MEN
PNEUM = the breath of life, spirit, presence giving life to man, acknowledged by the ability, the divine power to make conscious choice: assent, agree to, or command something and which uses, as a tool, MEN (see below) that mental capacity of remembrance (that remains with us), which can be love, madness, prayer, advice but which by its very nature continually projects (intrudes) its solo, isolated course into our midst.

    = MEN (PIE): to think > states of mind, thought = MIND, MEMORY, MENTAL, MENTION, MENTAL, MENTION, COMMENT, REMINISCE, MENTOR
    = MEN-TI (Teut.) = MINNA: love
    = MANIA (Grk.): madness = MANIAC > one who is mad > seer
    = MANTRA (Sanskrit): counsel, prayer, hymn
    = MON = MONERE (Lat.): remind, warn, advise
    = ADMONISH, SUMMON, MONITOR
      MEN: to project > jut, threaten = MENACE, PROMINENT
    = MONS (Grk.): MOUNTAIN
MEN: to REMAIN—MANERE (Lat.) = MANOR, MANSION, PERMANENT
MEN: small, isolated, alone = MONOS (Grk.): single = MONO-, MONK
THUS, MEN is that mental capacity of remembrance (that remains with us) that can be love, madness, prayer, advice, but which by its very nature continually projects (intrudes) its solo, isolated course into our midst (see MED, page xxx).

OS = AZ: he who or that which or one that

PHENOMENON = BHA-MEN-AZ: that which, by the force of its own appearance, projects, intrudes into our lives and conceptions, showing and demonstrating something about itself to our minds; BUT there is also required someone, continually pursuing his mad solo course, who has that durable mental capacity, prayer, madness, or love, which projects, intrudes into our lives and thinking, showing this something by both speech and action. A PHENOMENON exists objectively although some seer or witness must be present to direct attention toward it.

NOUMENON = GNO-MEN-AZ: that which is pointed out to us through various means of communication by he who:
    (1) having that durable mental capacity, prayer, madness, love
    (2) and continually pursuing his mad solo course,
    (3) sees, notices, understands and knows the inner meanings of what is seen,
    (4) and projects, intrudes into our lives and thinking, in order to so point them out.

A NEUMENON (meaning) cannot exist independent of the subjective understandings communicated by a human knower: a GNOSTIC—the finger pointing to the moon. But never confuse the finger with the moon.

THUS, NUMEN/PNEU-MEN: The divine presence, spirit, ever-present within man uses that durable mental capacity, prayer, madness, or love; and by its very nature projects, intrudes its solo isolated course into our inner life. AND when we become aware and awaken, we accept the power of conscious choice, will, and then the divine presence, being now actualized, realized, projects, intrudes itself out into the world.

Both PHENO-MEN-ON and NEU-MEN-ON have in common
    1.   MEN, which is the capacity, tool, to MENTATE; but also
    2.   the necessity of CONSCIOUS awareness of the -ON:-OS:-AZ: THAT.

So although we use PHENOMENON to mean objective truth as distinguished from the inner meaning NEUMENON, yet we now know (from physics) that even the description of an external event is dependent on the subjectivity of the observer. Thus "observation" is a continuum from the easiest seen properties of something to the most difficult abstractions of wisdom.

It is the more observant seer who sees, notes, and notices things about something and points them out to mankind—first to himself and later in language.

Then PHENO- and PNEU- are the two polarities on a continuum of observation, where PHENO- indicates the pragmatic, exoteric, surficial, and easier; and PNEU-, the ethical, esoteric, mystical, deeper, and more difficult. But in the vast gray area of the middle, there is no difference between them at all. The true picture is

PHENOMENON/MEDIUM/NEUMENON

The finger pointing to the moon is not the moon. We are here to be on the path. Some may be capable of reaching the neumenon and relating that to us, but that capability can only be reached by staying on THEWAY, which lies straight down the middle (medium— no amount of effort can make a finger into a moon). And he who is installed high up on the signpost finds it impossible to take even the smallest step on the way.

EPILOGUE

THAT "Entity"?
WHO? will it be?
Does the dichotomy exist?
Is there an identity,
or is it an illusion, fictitious,
a fake facade, a lie?

Or is this concept of "center" the one
that is an illusion, fictitious,
a fake, the lie?

Unfortunately, both can't be real.

If you are a modern atheist, scientist, or existentialist, you must (to be consistent) deny the existence of any kind of Christ-center, God as being merely ethereal hopes, desires, dreams, fantasies.

If, on the other hand, you want to believe in a God, Christ, etc., then you are forced to see the truth about yourSelf.

And you can't have it both WAYS.

WHO? knows what the right answer is.
Certainly, "you" don't.

Have ye not known?
Have ye not heard?
Hath it not been told you from the beginning?
Have ye not understood from the foundations of the earth?
—Isaiah 40:21

WATCH IT, Narcissus.